Project Zero Trust

Project Zero Trust

A Story about a Strategy for Aligning Security and the Business

George Finney

WILEY

More Wiley Books for Cybersecurity Leaders

Cyber Breach Response That Actually Works: Organizational Approach to Managing Residual Risk by Andrew Gorecki

Cybersecurity and Third-Party Risk: Third Party Threat Hunting by Gregory C. Rasner

How to Measure Anything in Cybersecurity Risk by Douglas W. Hubbard and Richard Seiersen

Navigating the Cybersecurity Career Path by Helen E. Patton

The Security Culture Playbook: An Executive Guide To Reducing Risk and Developing Your Human Defense Layer by Perry Carpenter and Kai Roer

Transformational Security Awareness: What Neuroscientists, Storytellers, and Marketers Can Teach Us About Driving Secure Behaviors by Perry Carpenter

Tribe of Hackers Security Leaders: Tribal Knowledge from the Best in Cybersecurity Leadership by Marcus J. Carey and Jennifer Jin

You CAN Stop Stupid: Stopping Losses from Accidental and Malicious Actions by Ira Winkler and Tracy Celaya Brown

To Amanda and Story

Contents

About the Author   xi

Acknowledgments   xiii

Foreword   xv

Introduction   xxi

Chapter 1:   The Case for Zero Trust   1

Key Takeaways   10

Chapter 2:   Zero Trust Is a Strategy   13

Key Takeaways   26

    The Four Zero Trust Design Principles   27

    The Five-Step Zero Trust Design Methodology   27

    The Zero Trust Implementation Curve   27

Chapter 3:   Trust Is a Vulnerability   29

Key Takeaways   39

Chapter 4:   The Crown Jewels   43

Key Takeaways   54

Chapter 5:   The Identity Cornerstone   57

Key Takeaways   71

Chapter 6:   Zero Trust DevOps   73
Key Takeaways   83

Chapter 7:   Zero Trust SOC   87
Key Takeaways   100

Chapter 8:   Cloudy with a Chance of Trust   103
Key Takeaways   113

Chapter 9:   A Sustainable Culture   117
Key Takeaways   129

Chapter 10:   The Tabletop Exercise   133
Key Takeaways   147

Chapter 11:   Every Step Matters   151
Key Takeaways   159

Appendix A: Zero Trust Design Principles and Methodology   165
The Four Zero Trust Design Principles   165
The Five-Step Zero Trust Design Methodology   166

Appendix B: Zero Trust Maturity Model   167

Appendix C: Sample Zero Trust Master Scenario Events List   171

Appendix D: For Further Reading   179
Standards, Frameworks, and Other Resources   179
Case Studies   180
Google BeyondCorp Papers   180
Books   181
Hardening Guides   181

Glossary   183
Index   191

About the Author

George Finney is a Chief Information Security Officer who believes that people are the key to solving our cybersecurity challenges. George is the bestselling author of several cybersecurity books, including the award-winning book *Well Aware: Master the Nine Cybersecurity Habits to Protect Your Future* (Greenleaf Book Group Press, 2020). George was recognized in 2021 as one of the top 100 CISOs in the world by CISOs Connect. He has worked in cybersecurity for over 20 years and has helped startups, global telecommunications firms, and nonprofits improve their security posture. George is also an attorney, but don't hold that against him.

Acknowledgments

I couldn't have written this book without the help of a huge number of people who were willing to take their time and share their expertise with me. I'd first like to thank my friend and mentor, John Kindervag, for his help throughout my career as I took my organization through our Zero Trust journey and as I developed this story.

I also owe a debt of gratitude to my publisher, Jim Minatel, who not only believed in the project, but that I could actually somehow pull it off. And I'd like to thank the team at Wiley and Sons, particularly John Sleeva, Pete Gaughan, and Melissa Burlock for their invaluable contributions to make this book what it is.

Cybersecurity is a team sport. We can't do what we do without sharing our experiences with one another. When I picked up my phone and began asking for help, the community came together and answered the call. I'd like to personally thank Zach Vinduska for being right there with me all the way through the creation of the book. I'd also like to thank Adam Shostack for his insights and helping make all of the details come to life.

I'd also like to give a huge shout out to my friends and colleagues Jason Fruge, Helen Patton, Eve Maler, Russ Kirby, Rob LaMagna-Reiter, Exodus Almasude, Chase Cunningham, Josh Danielson, Jordan Mauriello, Malcolm Harkins, and Steve King. I consider myself incredibly lucky to know all of you.

And, finally, I'd like to thank my wife Amanda and my daughter Story for their support, their inspiration, and their understanding while I pursued my dream of being a writer.

—George Finney

Foreword

When my friend George Finney told me he was going to write a novel about Zero Trust, my initial response was, "Why?" The idea that anyone would want to read a novel about Zero Trust, let alone write one, was a bit of a head-scratcher. Gratifying, to be sure, but still bizarre. You see, when I first created the concept of Zero Trust, folks thought I was crazy. Not just quirky crazy, like so many of us in IT and cybersecurity, but genuinely insane crazy.

I have spent many years trying to convince people to be open-minded enough to consider building Zero Trust environments. The notion that someone wanted to write a book of fiction revolving around an idea I had created was mind-blowing. So that's how George ended up sitting on my living room sofa while I told him the story of how Zero Trust came to be.

To understand Zero Trust, you must first understand the origins of cybersecurity. "Cybersecurity" is a relatively new term. Before that, we called it "information security"—a much better name (what's a cyber and why should it be secured?). And before that, there was network security, because networks were the first type of Internet technology that needed securing. For years, networks were being built in universities and the occasional rogue, cutting-edge company, but there were no threats—hence, no built-in security. In fact, TCP/IP v4, which we all know and love, wasn't developed until 1983. Therefore, there were all these researchers and visionaries salivating about how the "Internet" could be used and monetized. No one was even thinking about the possibility that someone might want to attack these nascent networking systems.

Then, in 1983, an NSA computer scientist and cryptographer named Robert H. Morris testified before Congress, warning of network threats via a new phenomenon called "the computer virus." In one of the great cosmic ironies of the computer age, his son Robert Tappan Morris created arguably the first computer worm, the eponymous Morris worm, in 1988. The Morris worm infected between 2,000 and 6,000 machines, a massive number considering that the entire Internet had only about 60,000 computers connected to it. Depending on who you asked, the Morris worm caused between $100K and $10M in damages. Suddenly network security was hot.

Alas, no one knew how to secure a network, as no one was thinking about threats to the network. So a few enterprising and ambitious folks, of which I was not one, created products called "firewalls" and "antivirus software," sold them to various companies and organizations, and became very wealthy in the process.

Fast-forward to the turn of the century, and I installed firewalls for a living in the Dallas–Fort Worth area. The primary firewall I deployed was the PIX firewall by Cisco. The PIX firewall was ubiquitous and drove a lot of infosec thinking. Its core component was known as the Adaptive Security Algorithm, or ASA. Of course, there was nothing adaptive about it, and it offered very little security, but Cisco could market the heck out of it.

Step one of a PIX install was to set the "trust" levels on the interfaces. By default, the external interface to the Internet was "untrusted" with a "trust" level of 0, and the internal interface to the customer network was "trusted" with a "trust" level of 100. Typically several other interfaces were being used for DMZs (demilitarized zones), a term stolen from the Vietnam War that I guess sounded cool, where specific assets such as web or email servers were deployed. Those interfaces were given an arbitrary "trust" level between 1 and 99. So the "trust" level determined how a packet could flow through the PIX firewall. In their documentation, Cisco said:

> Adaptive Security follows these rules: Allow any TCP connections that originate from the inside network.

Because of the "trust" model, traffic—by default—can flow from a higher "trust" level (inside) to a lower "trust" level (outside of a DMZ) without a specific rule. This is very dangerous. Once an attacker gets purchase inside your network, no policy stops them from setting up a command and control channel or from exfiltrating data. This is a significant flaw in the technology, but, sadly, everyone seemed to be okay with it. When I would put in outbound rules, both clients and co-workers would get upset. "That's not the way it's supposed to be done!" I left many client sites dejected because it was self-evident to me that bad things were in store for the client.

So I learned to hate trust. Not trust between people, but "trust" in the digital realm. So I started studying the concept of trust, thinking about it, and asking questions like "why is 'trust' in digital systems?" It became clear that this "trust model" was broken and was the proximate cause of numerous data breaches.

I discovered that there are other problems linked to the "trust model." The first is the anthropomorphization of technology. To make complex digital systems more understandable, we've tried to humanize them through our language. For example, we say things like "George is on the network." Now I'm pretty sure that my friend George has never been on a network in his entire life. He has never been shrunken down into a subatomic particle and sent down a wire to some destination like an email server or the public Internet. This rarely ever happens in movies: in *Lawnmower Man* or *Tron*, but even in *The Matrix*, they have to plug in. But how do I tell this story?

Now, this is where fate intervened. I received a call from Forrester Research asking if I wanted to be an analyst. Sure! Although I didn't really know what an analyst was. But Forrester was a blessing. It gave me the freedom to ask questions. In our initial analyst training class, we were told that our mission was to "Think Big Thoughts." Right on, as George would say.

The first big thought I investigated was that injecting "trust" into digital systems was a stupid idea. I was now free to explore that contentious statement. There was no vendor or co-worker to put the kibosh on thinking. Freedom—that was the great gift that Forrester gave me.

Just a few months after joining Forrester, a vendor reached out and asked, "What's the wackiest idea you are working on?" I told him I wanted to eliminate the concept of trust from digital systems. It was all in. He had been looking for some radical notion to justify a golfing excursion he wanted to schedule.

So in the fall of 2008, I did a series of five events at five Scottish links–style courses in Montreal, Philly, Boston, New York, and Atlanta. At each course, I gave a presentation on this nascent idea that became "Zero Trust." Then we played a round of golf with the attendees. So many questions and great conversations.

Side note: I traveled with just my golf shoes and a big bag full of balls because I lost so many on those links courses.

Ahh, the memories. These were the first five Zero Trust speeches. So Zero Trust was born at a country club in Montreal. I wasn't sure where the research would lead, but I knew I was on to something after that first speech was over.

So began a two-year journey of primary research, talking to all kinds of people, CISOs, engineers, and cybersecurity experts that I admired. I asked for feedback. "Poke holes in the idea." Eventually, the only negative thing that was said was "That's not the way we've always done it." So I started testing the message in small speeches and webinars. There was a core group of people who got it. They became the original advocates.

In September 2010, I published the original Zero Trust Report: "No More Chewy Centers: Introducing the Zero Trust Model of Information Security." People read it, called up about it, and brought me out to give speeches and design networks around it.

Zero Trust is a new idea to many, but I have spent the last 14 years focused on it. Zero Trust has taken me around the world—to Asia, Europe, and the Middle East. It has introduced me to many of the great leaders and thinkers in the world. I've met with CEOs, board members, congresspeople, generals, admirals, and innumerable IT and cyber folks fighting the good fight against our digital adversaries. Not bad for a kid from a farm in rural Nebraska whose only goal was to *not* get up a 5 a.m. to feed cattle and irrigate corn.

It's gratifying to see so many individuals give speeches and write papers and even books on Zero Trust. I've advised students who are writing their master's thesis or doctoral dissertations on Zero Trust. I tried to write a book myself, but it's hard to do the work and then write about it simultaneously.

The penultimate moment came in 2021, when President Joe Biden issued his executive order on improving cybersecurity in the federal government, which mandates that all federal agencies move toward adopting a Zero Trust architecture. If you had told me a decade ago that this would happen, I would've told you to get back in your DeLorean and accelerate it up to 88 mph because that would never happen. But it did, and it's changed everything. Primarily it has inverted the incentive structure. It used to be that only the radicals inside an organization were Zero Trust advocates. Now, it's okay to adopt Zero Trust because of President Biden. He moved the needle.

But the most satisfying moment in my career came when a young man saw me on a plane and came up to where I was seated. He handed me his business card with the title "Zero Trust Architect" printed on it. He reached out his hand and said, "Thank you, I have a job because of you." Wow.

So, thank you, George, for being a steadfast friend and Zero Trust advocate. Thanks for writing this book and all the crazy creativity you apply to this crazy business. Cybersecurity needs more George Finneys.

—John Kindervag, SVP, Cybersecurity Strategy at ON2IT

Introduction

The most effective means we have available to protect ourselves when it comes to cybersecurity is prevention. And the most effective strategy for prevention is Zero Trust. To be successful at any endeavor, you need a strategy. Many organizations struggle with success when it comes to cybersecurity—not because they are doing nothing but because they don't have a consistent strategy for protecting their data. Zero Trust is a strategy for protecting your organization's most important assets. This strategy focuses on preventing breaches by eliminating one of your biggest blind spots when it comes to computers and computer networks—trust.

Zero Trust is the bridge between the unique goals of your business and the specific tactics needed to secure the business. A 2020 report by Okta indicates that 60 percent of organizations in North America are currently working on Zero Trust projects, and President Biden has issued an executive order to federal agencies to implement Zero Trust in government.

Project Zero Trust puts readers in the driver's seat on a journey to transform the security of a recently breached company by taking them through each step of implementing Zero Trust. The book follows the story of Dylan, who hasn't even started his job as Director of Infrastructure at his new job the company when the organization finds itself a victim of ransomware. While the CIO handles the breach response and investigation, Dylan is charged with transforming the company using John Kindervag's Zero Trust design methodology. Readers will be able to take these lessons back to their own organizations and have actionable examples that they can apply to specific roles and situations at their organizations.

Readers will learn:

- John Kindervag's five-step methodology for implementing Zero Trust
- The four Zero Trust design principles
- How to limit the blast radius of a breach
- How to align security with the business
- Common myths and pitfalls when implementing Zero Trust
- Implementing Zero Trust in cloud environments

Since Zero Trust focuses on a strategy of prevention, readers will find opportunities to realize improvements in efficiency and reduced costs, in addition to increased security.

Project Zero Trust is essential for both aspiring technology professionals as well as experienced IT leaders, network engineers, system administrators, and project managers who need to implement Zero Trust initiatives in their organizations. *Project Zero Trust* demonstrates how Zero Trust can be integrated into any organization using easy-to-understand examples, bridging the gap between technical reference guides, vendor marketing, and organizational strategy.

Project Zero Trust

Chapter 1
The Case for Zero Trust

It was still dark in the room, but Dylan couldn't sleep any longer. He looked at the clock. It was only 4:45—not enough time to go back to sleep but too early to actually get up. Dylan was starting a new job today. Maybe his dream job if things worked out. So what if he was a little anxious? He was also genuinely excited, and he hadn't felt that way about a job in a long time. Or maybe ever. He closed his eyes again hoping for another few minutes of sleep.

Dylan opened his eyes and turned back to the clock. It now read 4:46. He decided to get up instead of waiting for the alarm. His house slippers sat next to his running shoes in front of the nightstand. He slipped on his running shoes. He turned on the lamp and walked to the treadmill sitting on the opposite side of the room. He grabbed his right ankle with his right hand, stretching his quadricep, stretched the other leg, then hopped onto the treadmill.

He heard the warm tone of recognition as the treadmill scanned his face and loaded his profile. His three favorite workouts popped up on the curved LED screen. He tapped the fourth icon at the bottom, and he could see nine livestreams of runners from across the world. He picked the one on a beach in Costa Rica and began running. He could hear a whoop from several other runners following the livestream that he had gone on runs with before as they saw him join.

But then a funny thing happened: the livestream froze. Then instead of reconnecting him, the treadmill started to slow down to a safe speed, then stopped. The March Fitness logo appeared on the screen like when his Wi-Fi had gone out a few months back. Dylan stepped off the treadmill and checked his phone, but the Wi-Fi seemed to be working.

He decided to jump in the shower and start getting ready for work. After he had gotten dressed, he started his morning ritual of making his coffee and checking his email for any news alerts. Since he was starting at a new company, he had created an alert to send him an email whenever a news story about his new company, March Fitness, and the word "IT" or "outage" were mentioned. To his horror, his inbox was full of emails. His treadmill wasn't the only one that wasn't working. The whole company was down due to an outage. Worse, a cybersecurity reporter was claiming on Twitter that the company had just experienced a widespread cyberattack.

Dylan stood there, unable to move. How could this be happening? On his first day? An alarm was going off somewhere, and it took Dylan a moment to realize that it was his alarm clock. It was finally time for him to wake up.

There was still a chill in the air as Dylan ran up the steps of the headquarters building. In the center of the stairs was a giant running shoe made from a wire mesh with only the toe of the shoe attached to the slab of marble underneath. He walked through the revolving door, and more wire mesh shoes divided the length of the hallway, each in slightly different running positions, as though some giant had just run through, losing a new shoe at each point in its stride. The lobby to the headquarters of March Fitness ran the entire length of the building, separating the headquarters of the company into the north side and the south side.

The north side of the building is where all the executives of the company had their offices, along with marketing, HR, finance, and sales. The south side of the building was where the Information Technology offices were located, along with the research and development offices. Unlike when he had interviewed, there was no one at the security desk, and the security doors on either side of the building were propped wide open. There was a steady stream of what Dylan thought were interns sprinting north to south and south to north, all carrying crumpled up papers in either hand. This was a bad sign; if they had resorted to physical messengers, it meant that not only email was down but also instant messaging and the phone system. Or maybe they had taken the network itself down to prevent the attack from spreading further?

Since Dylan didn't know where he should report, he headed toward the south side because that was where he had interviewed. He naturally broke into a jog to keep up with the messengers, and although he was in good shape and his six-foot-two-inch frame meant his steps were longer than average, the messengers darted around him like he was standing still.

He passed a bank of elevators and went into a cubicle farm where 100 employees would have normally sat. Instead, all the monitors were dark, and each had a piece of paper taped to it that read, "Do not power on."

He followed the stream of breathless messengers to a conference room where he finally saw someone he recognized. Dr. Noor Patel, the Chief Information Officer, was sitting at the head of a conference table in the center of the room. Noor was wearing a black suit and white shirt, with her trademark black silk tie. At the opposite side of the table was Olivia Reynolds, the CEO and Founder of March Fitness. Everyone else at the table was wearing suits except for Reynolds, who was wearing one of March Fitness's own brand of running suit.

"Dylan?" a woman whispered into his ear. She had silently moved through the standing-room-only crowd that had gathered around the meeting and startled Dylan. She had dark hair and was almost as tall as Dylan and smelled like lilacs. She was holding a binder full of papers that read *Business Continuity Plan*.

"I'm Isabelle. . . I run the Project Management Office. Noor asked me to keep an eye out for you this morning. Heck of a first day." She turned to stand next to Dylan and watch the discussion going on at the center of the room.

She handed him his ID card, the retractable holder already attached. "You're lucky we printed this last week. Now the whole card reader system is down, just like everything else. We started seeing some unusual activity on the network sometime Sunday evening," Isabelle whispered to Dylan. "By this morning, things were out of control."

He pinned the ID card to his belt, "I'm guessing you guys took the network down as a precaution? Do they know what the cause is?"

"Good guess, Dylan. Actually, a number of computers seem to have been infected with ransomware. We're still investigating the cause, but the company is losing money every minute the network is down, so what they're focusing on now is the fastest way to get us back online."

Olivia Reynolds spoke softly, but everyone immediately stopped talking and turned to look at her. "How do we know this ransom isn't just some kind of scam?" she asked. "Even if we did pay them, how do we know they'll actually unlock our computers?"

"Ma'am," one of the suits next to Noor spoke up. Unlike Noor, his suit was wrinkled and didn't seem to fit quite right. "We see this issue come up frequently. There are scam ransomware actors out there. We can tell when this is the case, because they'll use the same bitcoin wallet for all their victims. In those cases, you'll see lots of transactions where their victims tried to pay up."

"That's our security consultant, Peter Liu," Isabelle clarified quietly to Dylan.

"And in our case?" Olivia asked.

"In our case," Noor responded before the consultant could answer, "the bitcoin wallet is brand new, with only one transaction that we believe was just the cybercriminal testing the account."

"How does that explain anything?" asked a white-haired man wearing a blue pinstripe suit.

"That's our General Counsel, Kofi Abara," Isabelle clarified. "He's one of the smartest people I've ever met. Also, he runs a monthly poker tournament. He was actually in the World Series of Poker a few years ago. Never bet against him."

"It's an accounting issue," Peter explained. "The cybercriminal needs to know which victims have paid and which haven't. The only way to do that is to have a different bitcoin wallet for each victim. Seeing that the bitcoin wallet is empty means this cybercriminal is serious."

"What's our next move?" Olivia asked.

Noor stood up and addressed the room. "We aren't going to pay this cybercriminal if we can avoid it. We have our backups, and our team will go into overtime bringing computers back online from scratch. We've delayed upgrading our antivirus to a more modern EDR solution, so we'll be doing these upgrades in parallel while we restore our devices. This will improve our visibility into systems to be able to detect and prevent further intrusions as well. Our consultants will be working with us to ensure the entire process will take hours, not days." There were cheers from around the room from nervous IT staff ready to get to work.

Isabelle leaned over to Dylan and asked, "What's an EDR tool?"

"It's like antivirus software on steroids," Dylan whispered. "It stands for endpoint detection and response. Old antivirus programs would use a kind of fingerprint to find malware, but the bad guys figured this out and would use different fingerprints. EDR works like facial recognition, so it doesn't matter if you grow a beard or put on glasses. It can also take action to kick the bad guys out."

Isabelle nodded thoughtfully as the conversation in the room settled back down.

"That sounds like a great plan, Dr. Patel, but what if it takes longer than you expect?" Kofi asked.

"Our cyber risk insurance company will continue negotiating with the cybercriminals on our behalf," said a blonde woman wearing a bright red suit. She nodded to several consultants who were standing up behind her. "They'll be working with the ransomware gang to reduce the ransom as though we intended to pay, to buy us additional time."

"That's Kim Self," Isabelle added. "She's our Chief Risk Officer. I'll introduce you later." Noor spoke up again, this time flanked by two directors who had been taking her notes down on their notepads.

"If our restoration goes for more than 36 hours," Noor clarified, "working in shifts, then we'll recommend paying the ransom. But we expect to be fully operational again in three days."

"How much will that hurt?" Olivia asked, turning to look in Dylan's direction.

Dylan was startled when the pink-haired woman standing on the other side of him answered. "We'll be giving a free month of credit to all of our subscribers for the outage." Dylan could see her nametag read *Donna Chang, Chief Financial Officer*. "It will hurt the same whether it's a day or a week. We can handle it for now, but we need to start thinking about the long term. Customer melt is a concern. But frankly the bigger concern will be the recovery costs, which are still unknown."

Olivia stood up and addressed the room, "Thank you all for being here. I'm not going to lie, the coming days will be a challenge. We will get through this challenge. We will be stronger because of it. We'll meet back here at the same time tomorrow, and we'll keep the video conference going so check in if you have any updates before then. Also, make sure you have the cell phone numbers for the people on your team until we can get our phone system back."

The next several hours were a blur as Dylan worked to help whomever he could. But with no access and not much information about the network, there wasn't much he could do. He mostly became a gopher, picking up supplies and carrying them to admins scrambling to rebuild computers from scratch.

"There you are," said Isabelle, who was peeking over a cubicle wall. Dylan was under the desk, unplugging it to bring to an admin he was working with. He hit his head on the bottom of the desk as he came out.

"Please tell me you've got something for me to do? I've been carrying around computers all morning."

"Boss needs you." She was already walking away at a brisk pace, and Dylan had to run to catch up.

She took him back out into the lobby, past a giant sneaker suspended in mid-air, and into the north side of the building.

Dylan's phone buzzed in his pocket. He pulled it out. It was Chuck, the recruiter whom he had worked with to get the job here at MarchFit. He silenced the call and kept following.

The smell of espresso filled the air of the executive suite. It made Dylan feel even more alert than he already was. "Is that the original stand-up desk treadmill that Olivia invented?" Dylan asked as they passed several prototype desk and treadmill concepts before the TreadMarch+ that Dylan owned came out.

They walked by a tall conference room table that had small treadmills where each of the chairs would have been. "Walking meetings," Isabelle said. "We had several large clients ready to place orders before the pandemic hit."

Isabelle turned to smile at him, but kept walking. They arrived at a pair of bright orange double doors. Isabelle knocked and opened the door for Dylan.

He walked in, but Isabelle didn't follow. "Best of luck" was all she said as she walked away.

The office was framed by two walls of glass with a TreadMarch+ stand-up desk facing the windows. The third wall looked like a NASCAR garage, with red tool chests and work benches covered with power tools and treadmill parts in pieces scattered everywhere. In the center of the room was a small white table surrounded by four red, modern-looking couches. On the table was a stack of several binders. The one on top was the same one Dylan had seen Isabelle carrying earlier, the Business Continuity Plan.

"Is this the guy?" said an unfamiliar gentleman sitting on one of the couches. Olivia's office, Dylan finally realized. Noor was sitting with her arms folded across from Olivia, who was leaning on the top of her desk. Noor nodded yes in answer to the man's question.

"Tell me, Mr. Thomas, do you believe that the incident that just happened to MarchFit could have been prevented?"

Dylan looked to Noor and Olivia. Their faces were blank, apparently waiting for him to answer. This was a serious question.

"I don't really know enough about all our technology to answer . . ." Dylan responded, but was interrupted.

"This isn't a technical question. This is a philosophical question. Do you believe that prevention is possible?" The man had tented his fingers waiting for Dylan to respond.

"I suppose," Dylan began, "that we have to believe prevention is possible."

The man waited several seconds for Dylan to continue, then asked, "Why do you have to believe that prevention is possible, Mr. Thomas?"

"Don't you have to believe that success is possible in order to have success? If we didn't believe we could prevent cybercriminals from breaking in, we'd unconsciously make it happen. Also, I'd be crazy for making this my career and not believe I could make a difference."

"Next question. What's the purpose of cybersecurity?" the man asked, folding his arms.

Dylan considered. "Security is only here to enable the business to keep running smoothly." The man nodded wisely at this and was silent for a long time. "Was there another question?" Dylan asked, turning to Noor and Olivia.

"Last question," the man said. "Do you enjoy learning?"

"Sure," Dylan answered. "You have to love learning in IT. We're always learning about the next new advance in technology."

The man jumped up from his seat quickly, and before he knew it, Dylan was shaking his hand. "You're about to learn a lot," he said to Dylan. "He'll do," he said to Olivia and Noor, and began walking out the door. "I'll see you tomorrow, Mr. Thomas."

"I'm sorry about all of this, Dylan," Noor said, turning to Olivia. She sat down on the couch where the man had just been sitting and gestured for Dylan to sit across from her. Olivia sat down next to Noor.

"There's nothing to apologize for," Olivia countered. She turned to Dylan, beaming. "This is a huge opportunity, Dylan. I'm really glad to meet you. I usually meet all our employees, but I wish we were meeting under different circumstances."

"We could at least ask him first so that he knows what he's getting into," Noor said. "Dylan, I know you were planning on meeting your team today."

"I saw a couple of them already," Dylan responded.

"Yes. But obviously some things have come up," Noor said. "Don't worry, you're not being fired or anything. But since you've not been trained yet, or really had any orientation time, you're not going to be much help with the incident response." She picked up her coffee cup and took a long, slow drink.

"Now it sounds like I'm being fired," Dylan laughed nervously.

"Dylan," Olivia answered, "you're definitely not being fired. A few hours ago, I asked Dr. Patel here what the most cutting-edge security program was in the world. And Dr. Patel, you said?"

"Zero Trust," Noor answered.

"Do you know what Zero Trust is, Dylan?" Olivia asked.

He folded his arms and crossed his legs. "I've heard of it, but I don't know much about it. Isn't that just a marketing term for security companies?"

The two women looked at each other with a knowing glance. Dylan got the uneasy feeling that this conversation had happened already.

"I asked the question, and it turns out that one of the world's foremost experts on Zero Trust lives just a few minutes away from us," Olivia explained. "You just met him. He's worked with John Kindervag and Dr. Chase Cunningham, the two Forrester analysts who pioneered Zero Trust. His name is Aaron Rapaport, by the way, but I don't think he actually introduced himself."

"So, I'll be what, working for him now?" Dylan asked.

"Technically, you'll still be working for me," Noor corrected.

Dylan turned his head to the side. "Technically?"

"She means that for the next six months you'll have a dotted line reporting directly to me," Olivia said.

"Oh" was all Dylan could manage. "So this consultant is my Obi-Wan? He'll teach me the ways of Zero Trust?"

"Here's why I'm convinced Zero Trust will work for us," Olivia said, both to Dylan as well as to Noor. "I read that the president has issued an executive order requiring the government to adopt Zero Trust as a strategy for securing the government against other governments. When I talked to Aaron just now, he convinced me. Dylan, tell me why I'm convinced."

"If the government is adopting it, then it must be right?" Dylan said sarcastically. The three of them burst into laughter. Noor finally relaxed in her seat.

"No. I was convinced because it's actually a strategy for security. This is the issue that Noor and I have been debating. With any other goal or objective in our business, we've got a strategy for achieving it. Our goal in security is to prevent bad things from happening. I know we can go buy tools or implement more tech to add to security, but how do we know we're on the right track? In every other area of the business we have a strategy, and Zero Trust is going to be our security strategy moving forward."

"I'll be leading the incident response and recovery efforts," Noor explained. "But at the same time, we'll be launching a transformation initiative for all of the technology in the company to fully implement Zero Trust."

"You've heard that an ounce of prevention is worth a pound of cure?" Olivia asked Dylan. He nodded. "That's what I expect of Zero Trust. That's why Aaron asked you about whether you believe in prevention. We believe that prevention is the most efficient way of stopping breaches, and Zero Trust is the best strategy for implementing prevention in technology."

"That makes sense," Dylan said.

"This is a huge career opportunity. You'll be in charge of implementing Zero Trust at a company that's a household name. It would be crazy to turn this down," Olivia said, looking at Noor.

"So what happens in six months?" Dylan asked. "You said I'd just be reporting to you for six months?"

"In six months, we'll be launching a whole new product that will change the way the world looks at fitness, work-life balance, everything. We can't afford to make a misstep that could keep us from being first to market," Olivia said.

"We won't take for granted that you are on board with this new challenge, Dylan," Noor said. "You should take some time to think about this. You've specialized in managing IT infrastructure your whole career, and this is a different kind of challenge, and not one that you thought you had signed up for yesterday. I wouldn't expect you to just blindly accept an offer like this."

There was a soft knock at the door and a redheaded woman wearing a yellow suit came in without waiting for an answer. "Oh good, you're both here," she said as she approached Olivia and Noor. "We got a hit from our media monitoring service. The hacker has gone public with his demands." She handed her phone to Olivia, while Noor and Dylan came closer so that the three of them could see the tweet from the cybercriminal.

A tweet from the cybercriminal 3nc0r3 publicly threatening MarchFit and confirming rumors of a cyberattack

"Dylan, this is April, our head of public relations," Noor said. April reached out and shook Dylan's hand.

"Who is this Encore person?" Olivia asked.

"His profile makes it seem like he's based somewhere in Eastern Europe or Russia, but it's not clear where he's from. His past tweets indicate he's ransomed several other organizations, but we're the biggest target he's gone after so far," April explained, taking back her phone.

"I'll check with the negotiator to see if this is the same person they've been talking to," Noor said, standing up. "The negotiator was supposed to be stalling for more time. This could change our timeline." She walked to the door, and Dylan followed before she stopped him. "You can take all the time you need to think about this, so long as you make your decision in the next few hours." She winked at him. "Also, if you decide to be our Zero Trust project leader, you're going to have a bit of homework before tomorrow." Noor pointed to the stack of binders on the table.

Dylan began to walk outside. He was carrying one of Olivia's designer backpacks heavy with all the paperwork he had to read. On the way out the door, he noticed MarchFit's motto, "Every Step Matters," written above the entrance to the building. The fresh air helped, but what he really needed was to go for a run. The stress usually just melted away when he ran.

The job he'd be doing wasn't like anything he'd ever done before. It was an opportunity, but not the one he had been imagining just a few hours ago.

He unlocked his phone and remembered he had missed a call. He hadn't noticed that there was a voicemail, so he pressed the button and put the phone to his ear.

"Dylan, this is Chuck. Man, I know you just started over there at MarchFit and I heard about the breach. I just heard back from one of the other companies you were interviewing with at the same time as MarchFit and they're making you an offer. Dylan, it's more money and you'd be in a very similar role. If you think this thing is going south, give me a call and we can get you out of there."

Dylan collapsed onto the bench, exhausted. Things were moving too fast. He was too tired to think straight.

He looked up and saw a couple running together past the building. They waved as they passed by. Then more people ran. He realized the running trails that surrounded the headquarters building were full of runners. They were hooting their support every time one of the exhausted MarchFit employees would leave the building.

He hit the button to call Chuck.

"Dylan, hey buddy. I knew you'd be calling. You don't need to let this job set you back. . . ."

"Chuck, thanks for the offer, but I'm going to see this one through."

"Are you sure, man? Some companies don't do so well after a breach. I'm talking layoffs. I'm giving you a safe way out, bro. You could go be a director of cloud infrastructure anywhere. You're on your way to being a CIO soon. I'm worried this could hold you back."

"March Fitness got me through the pandemic, Chuck. You knew me three years ago. If I hadn't gotten that treadmill, I might not be here. I'm serious, losing all that weight has made a difference for me. I know it can make a difference for other people, and I'm going to stick it out here to make sure the company is still here to help other people."

Key Takeaways

Trust is a vulnerability.

Zero Trust is a cybersecurity strategy that says that the fundamental problem we have is a broken trust model where the untrusted side of the network is the evil Internet and the trusted side is the stuff we control. Therefore, organizations don't do any real security on the trusted side. However, almost all data breaches and negative cybersecurity events are an exploitation of that broken trust model. Zero Trust is about getting rid of trust when it comes to technology. How much trust should you have in a digital system? The answer is zero. Hence, Zero Trust.

Zero Trust is a strategy for success when it comes to cybersecurity. The reason that Zero Trust resonates with presidents, CEOs, and other leaders is that they recognize that having a strategy for winning in any discipline is critical to success. Every company is different, which means that how a strategy is implemented will vary from one company to the next. A successful Zero Trust implementation will be custom tailored for each business to meet their unique needs, tools, and processes.

The primary goal of Zero Trust is to prevent breaches. Prevention is possible. In fact, it's more cost effective from a business perspective to prevent a breach than it is to attempt to recover from a breach, pay a ransom, and deal with the costs of downtime or lost customers.

Zero Trust is more than just a marketing buzzword. Zero Trust isn't any one specific tool that you can buy, because you can use many different tools to achieve the same objectives. Zero Trust isn't a reference architecture, because each implementation of Zero Trust will be completely customized.

Project Zero Trust will take you on the journey of a company that will successfully implement Zero Trust. You'll learn the most important concepts, methodologies, and design principles to take back to your own organization. For any strategy to work, you need to have some critical elements in place. March Fitness already had in place backups, a risk register, inventory, and a Business Continuity Plan (BCP) so they were able to recover rather than pay the ransom. They also had cyber risk insurance and already had contracts in place with a cybersecurity breach response service, and they were able to assist with the recovery and negotiations. And they had printed out all of their critical documentation on paper to ensure that it would be available even if their computers were offline. But even if you don't have these elements today, you can still adopt a strategy of Zero Trust.

Note that March Fitness has a Chief Information Officer (CIO) who also acts as their Chief Information Security Officer (CISO). Depending on the industry, many large organizations may or may not have a dedicated CISO or dedicated information security staff. Wherever your organization is at in its cybersecurity maturity, you can be successful at implementing a Zero Trust strategy. And if you haven't yet begun your Zero Trust journey, the best time to start is today.

Chapter 2
Zero Trust Is a Strategy

Dylan was walking quickly, trying to keep up with Aaron as he walked up the stairs to the executive briefing center. Dylan was carrying a backpack with all of the paper documentation he had received from Noor the day before. Behind them was a woman wearing jeans and a black hoodie and a tattered backpack whistling the opening riff from "Careless Whisper." Following her was a woman wearing cat-eye glasses and a vintage 1950s dress and carrying a leather satchel. A tall man wearing a polo shirt and a short man wearing a red Arsenal football jersey loitered behind, heads bowed down looking at their cell phones.

The briefing center was at the end of the lobby that separated north MarchFit from south MarchFit. The conference center was a free-standing island of steel and glass that appeared to float above the rest of the headquarters building lobby.

The smell of freshly brewed espresso greeted them as they walked through the entrance. Isabelle was sipping from a tiny coffee mug watching them. She lifted her espresso mug in salute to the group as they swiped their badges to enter the suite.

The IT incident response teams had taken over the south side conference rooms, trying to complete the remediation of all the computers that had been ransomed but also trying to piece together how the ransomware got in at all. The north side conference rooms were all taken by lawyers and marketing teams discussing the potential responses to the lawsuits that the company was facing. That left the Project Zero Trust team the luxury conference rooms usually reserved for meeting with the company's largest clients and investors.

"Your new laptop is on the table," Isabelle said to Dylan between sips of espresso.

"That's a good sign. Does that mean we're back in business?" Dylan asked.

"We're in good shape. They're bringing up parts of the network one by one. It sounds like we're actually ahead of schedule," Isabelle said.

"It's like an episode of *CSI* exploded all over the place," Harmony said, holding up a conference phone that could have been a small stealth drone. She set the phone down and ran to the small white box at the end of the room. "Is this a 3D printer?" she exclaimed. "Why would they need a 3D printer in a conference room?"

"It's so they can fabricate custom treadmill parts during meetings with clients," Isabelle explained. "It's the quietest 3D printer on the market."

"It's like being on *Star Trek*," said Harmony, touching the 20-foot-wide video wall that occupied the whole of the back wall of the conference room. As she touched it, the cursor responded, bringing up a welcome video on how to use the wall. "IT'S A TOUCH SCREEN?" she exclaimed.

Dylan began to address the group. "I'd like to thank you all in advance for all the hard work that we're about to put into this, well, we're calling it Project Zero Trust. And I'd like to introduce Aaron Rapaport, who. . . ."

"What's your strategy for success when it comes to security?" Aaron interrupted, addressing the whole conference room. He paused for several seconds waiting for someone to answer. "You guys do have a strategy, right?"

"From what I've heard so far, it sounds like MarchFit had a defense-in-depth approach to security," Dylan said defensively.

Aaron paused and took a deep breath. "Let's back up a bit, and start with what a strategy is. A strategy is like a plan on how to achieve a specific goal, right? So at the end, you'll know when you've reached your goal. Now, here's my question: How do you know when you've successfully achieved your goals with defense in depth?"

"Wouldn't you know when the number of successful attacks starts to go down?" Dylan answered.

"You don't control the number of attacks the bad guys send against you, and you may not always know whether they've been successful or not. How many layers do you need to keep the bad guys out? Eight? Ten? Twenty? This is why embracing defense in depth as your strategy really turns out to look a lot more like 'expense in depth.' There's no measure for success. And you're spending money you don't have on things you don't need to protect."

"What about our attack surface?" Dylan asked. "I've heard security people at conferences talking about shrinking the attack surface. Shouldn't we be doing that, too?"

Aaron laughed. "The whole world is your attack surface! Any person or device anywhere on the planet could unwittingly be used to attack you. Instead, with Zero Trust, we focus only on the things that we can control. This is why we shrink it down to something very small and easily known, like the 'protect surface.'"

"We've always had a best-of-breed strategy," said the woman in the hoodie.

"Who are you?" asked Aaron.

"Harmony Gold," she responded, and shook Aaron's hand. "I'm a network engineer."

"Harmony, lots of organizations use consultants or industry analysts to decide which are the best products to buy. This isn't a strategy, either. Having the best products doesn't stop organizations from getting breached. What really matters is making all those separate elements work together in one integrated system that is custom tailored to fit your unique business."

The sliding doors to the conference room whooshed open and the two men wearing polo shirts finally walked into the room, laughing. "The funeral is tomato!" said the taller of the two men, and then repeated the final point for emphasis, "Tomato!"

"I'm so glad you could join us today," Aaron said sarcastically. "Your company just experienced a breach and you're the team that's going to make sure it never happens again. So what's your strategy for making that happen?"

"Isn't there some list of best practices somewhere that we can just follow?" the tall man asked, taking his seat. And after a moment he added, "I'm Brent, by the way. This is Nigel. He's English." Nigel nodded and sat down.

"You didn't really specify which checklist you had in mind, Brent. But it doesn't matter, because compliance checklists aren't a strategy. There are some good tactics on those lists, but a lot of companies that were compliant got breached."

Nigel was showing Brent something on his cell phone. Harmony was staring out into the lobby watching the people walking north and south.

"What's going on with you guys?" Dylan asked. "Don't you guys realize how important Project Zero Trust is?"

"Sorry, Dylan," said the woman wearing cat-eye glasses. She was already sitting at the conference room table. Dylan hadn't realized she was there. "I thought this project was a punishment. Everyone else at the company is either working on the new product release or getting the company working again."

Nigel spoke up. "Sorry, mate, nobody wants us on their projects. So you're stuck with us."

"What do you guys do?" Dylan asked.

"I do identity," Brent said. "And Nigel here is one of the most underrated developers you'll ever get stuck with."

"I don't buy that for a minute," Dylan countered. "Getting the company back up and running is pretty urgent, but Project Zero Trust is going to change the company. And the six of us are going to be at the heart of that change. Noor wouldn't have selected y'all if she didn't have faith that we were exactly the right people for the job."

"Oh, and I should add that the PMO will push through any changes that the team recommends with immediate emergency change control," Isabelle added. "And our budget comes directly from Olivia, for what it's worth. It's not a blank check or anything, but it's as close as we'll ever get."

Aaron tapped on the video wall and a diagram of all of MarchFit's networks appeared on the wall. The treadmill network was depicted by a cloud in between two boxes, one marked *data center* and the other *treadmills*. Below that was a star-shaped network connecting various retail location icons with a building labeled *Headquarters*.

"The good news is that we don't need a blank check. Zero Trust is the best strategy we have for protecting MarchFit because it was purposefully created for preventing breaches. You've probably heard that an ounce of prevention is worth a pound of cure. We've studied organizations that have implemented Zero Trust, and we've shown that this focus on prevention really does create a tenfold decrease in cost and complexity. It might feel like leading a security incident response team is doing the 'real' security work, but I think it starts with people like you, doing the work of prevention every day."

"There are only nine things you need to know to do Zero Trust. Nine things. That's all. Anybody can remember nine things, I hope. Right?" Aaron pulled up a slide, displaying it next to the picture of the MarchFit network infrastructure:

1. Focus on business outcomes.
2. Design from the inside out.
3. Determine who/what needs access.
4. Inspect and log all traffic.

"There are four design principles and five steps to applying it. But the first of all the design principles is to focus on the business outcomes. If you don't know why you're doing something, you can't protect it. So how do you guys make money?"

"We sell subscriptions to our fitness network. And workout clothes. People love the clothes," the woman in the cat-eye glasses said.

"I didn't catch your name?" Aaron asked.

"It's Rose," she said quietly.

"Exactly, Rose. MarchFit is really a media company. You have a movie-quality studio, and the best athletes all over the world are your personal trainers. It's easy to think of yourselves as a company that makes treadmills with a desk attached to them. But your margins for hardware are very small. The reason that people love the company is the content."

"How exactly does that help us prevent a cybercriminal from getting in?" Brent asked.

"Just looking at the picture, you can tell that this network was designed from the outside in." Aaron pointed at the network diagram. "The detail in the picture focuses on the endpoints at the edge and then goes inward. That's why it fails, because we don't know what we're protecting."

"We just had a case of ransomware. Shouldn't we be focusing more on the endpoints at the edge?" Harmony asked.

"I heard from Noor this morning," Isabelle said, "that it's looking like the ransomware was installed by a user who had local admin privileges. You could just as easily argue it was a permissions issue," she said, folding her arms.

"This is why the third step we have is least privilege control access on a need-to-know basis," Aaron added. "Ask the question, does so-and-so need to have access to that data to get their job done? That's how I tell them. Don't use the words 'least privilege.' Say, 'Aaron, do you need that access to that data to do your job?' I'll bet most times the answer is no. We give too much access to too many people for no reason."

"I think we've all seen admin privileges given out to directors or executives as a status symbol instead of as a core part of their jobs," Dylan said.

Aaron nodded. "Then the fourth step is, inspect and log all that traffic, because in cases where we've seen there were rogue insiders or compromised accounts, no one looked at their packets post-authentication. We have this movement that Zero Trust equals identity and it doesn't. We're going to say that in the end, it consumes identity. You need to look at the packets post-authentication and see what they're doing. Is there attack traffic in there? Are they downloading thousands of documents? Are there hundreds of SSH connections outside the company? To even have a chance at detecting those anomalies, you need to have the data in the form of network or server logs."

"This is just a bunch of theory," Nigel interrupted. "When are we going to actually protect something?"

Aaron changed to the next slide, which had the following words:

1. Define the protect surface.
2. Map the transaction flows.
3. Architect a Zero Trust environment.

4. Create Zero Trust policies.
5. Monitor and maintain.

"I mentioned there were four design principles. But there is also a five-step methodology to applying those principles. I completely agree that it would be boring just to talk about the methodology, and it's better to just get some hands-on experience."

"Wait, we're going to start making changes now?" Dylan asked.

"We've got emergency authorization for any change we request," Isabelle confirmed. "If we put a request in it should be done within a few minutes."

"Don't worry, Dylan, we're not going to start with anything critical. The first step in the methodology is to define your protect surface. But at this point, we will only start with a learning protect surface." Aaron pulled up a slide with a line that looked like a wave. The bottom-left part of the wave was labeled "Learning" protect surfaces. As the wave went up, it was labeled "Practice" protect surfaces. The crest of the wave was labeled "Crown Jewels," which are the most business-critical protect surfaces, with the Secondary and Tertiary protect surfaces further down the wave.

"The only way to eat an elephant is one bite at a time. Everybody thinks, 'Oh, how are we ever going to implement Zero Trust?' Our environment is big so we break it down into little sections. You take a big problem, and you break it down

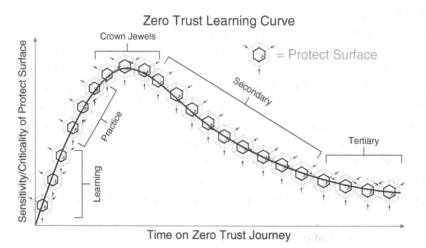

An organization's Zero Trust journey should begin with protecting several less-critical protect surfaces in order to prepare the team for success in more complex and critical protect surfaces later on.

Courtesy of ON2IT

into really small problems, and that's how you solve it. You can't do everything at once. That's why the first step in Zero Trust is to find the protect surfaces. You already know what these are. You've got your Business Continuity Plans and your Business Impact Assessments that tell you what the most important applications are in your environment."

"What about a basic application?" Brent asked. "Like DNS?"

"Your learning protect surface needs to be something that won't matter if we mess up," Aaron said. "DNS is definitely a business-critical application that we'll save for later."

"We have a SharePoint site for the training team. It's just an internal site for our team. It won't be a big deal if we take it down for a bit. Nobody will notice," said Rose.

"Perfect. Harmony, can you pull up the firewall rules for Rose's Share-Point site?"

Harmony connected her laptop to the video wall and began connecting to the terminal server with access to the management network. She pulled up a browser window with the firewall management application and searched for all the policies with the SharePoint label. A list of firewall policies came up showing the source port and address as well as the destination ports and addresses. Rose's server was at the end, labeled "Training Team."

"Every protect surface is bespoke," Aaron continued, "so each time you select a new protect surface, you need to follow this same methodology. This is the repeatable process for deploying Zero Trust. The second step for deploying Zero Trust in each protect surface is to map the transaction flows. I learned this the hard way. Early on, I was working on deploying some technology to a protect surface. There was a Windows 98 computer, and the client said to get rid of it since they couldn't possibly be running any production services there. Of course, it took everything down because it was the polling server between the point-of-sale terminals of about five thousand restaurants. As soon as you took it out, all these restaurants closed for the day because they couldn't process credit cards."

"What if the software documentation sucks?" Brent asked.

"This is one of the most common issues with implementing software with a Zero Trust approach," Aaron explained. "You only want to open the ports and the addresses needed and nothing else. I've seen documentation that tells you not to run a firewall at all. Some software guides don't tell you all the ports you'll need to open up, or sometimes they will tell you the wrong port numbers. Sometimes they don't document all the dependencies needed to harden a server, or they call on a library that we didn't know we needed as a prerequisite. You just need to keep in mind that all we're trying to do is create a micro-perimeter around a protect surface. You don't have to lock down everything inside the protect surface, because you're containing the blast radius to that protect surface."

"That makes sense," Dylan said.

"For some of the more critical applications, I'll actually recommend running packet captures. For new services, you might run all your traffic through a proxy in a test environment to show you all of the ports that are running," Aaron said. "But in this case, Dylan, can you run the netstat command on the server and show all the current running network connections?"

Dylan connected to the video wall and pulled up the server next to the window where Harmony was displaying the firewall rules and typed the netstat command. The server displayed a list of connected sessions currently running on the server, showing the protocol, source, and destination addresses. Harmony scrolled through the firewall policies to display the firewall rules so they were side by side with the output from the netstat command.

There were a number of firewall rules, each allowing different ports to be accessed on the SharePoint server.

"Does anyone notice what's wrong with this picture?" Aaron asked.

"The list of ports doesn't match up," Rose said. "The firewall policy allows a bunch of different ports to be open that aren't running on the server itself."

"This is more common than you think," Aaron observed. "Often servers will be decommissioned and new ones built with the same IP address. But no one tells the firewall admin, which it looks like may have been the case here. Dylan, take a note to review your server workflow process to look at decommissioning devices. Does anyone else see anything?"

"I don't understand," Harmony said. "All of the rules here are about what can talk to Rose's server, but there aren't any rules stopping Rose's server from talking out."

"Good catch, Harmony. This is one of the most common issues with how admins have configured firewalls for a long time. The idea was called a 'trust model,' and the way we trained firewall admins for years was that a server with high trust could always talk down to lower levels of trust with no restrictions. But, as we saw in the SolarWinds case and in all malware cases that have command and control, if you don't have a rule that specifies that this resource can only talk to these certain things, then it can—and will—talk to anything on the

Internet. There is never a time that any resource on your internal network should go outbound to an unknown server on the Internet. In Zero Trust, there's no concept of unknown traffic. If it is unknown, it should be blocked automatically by default. This is the problem. By allowing all outbound traffic, you're allowing malware to call out to their command and control networks. If you kill command and control, you're going to kill all this ransomware."

"You mean just a couple of firewall rules could have prevented this ransomware outbreak?" Nigel asked.

"Everyone wants to know what product to buy to do Zero Trust or to eliminate ransomware. The truth is that you won't know the answer to that until you've gone through the process. Which brings us to the third step in the methodology: architecting our Zero Trust environment. What protections do you have so far?"

Dylan spoke up. "There's endpoint protection already on the server, and there's a firewall in place. What else do we need?"

"This can get complicated quickly," Aaron said. "It sounds like there's already an out-of-band management system in place for the network devices and servers, which is essential. If this were a public SharePoint site, I might recommend adding a web application firewall, or WAF, to the architecture. But since this isn't a public SharePoint site, I'd actually prefer to just limit the server to talking internally."

"Rose, is that okay with you?" Dylan asked.

"There's actually some stuff there that isn't public. Can we make sure only people on my team have access?" Rose asked.

"Even better," Dylan said. "We can just create an address group for your team."

Aaron chuckled. "A lot of organizations limit access to sensitive servers by IP address so that you can only connect to a server from some secret server admin's desktop. But this isn't Zero Trust. It turns out in practice that attackers are very good at figuring out where those holes are. I'd prefer making a rule based on your role in the organization. Brent, is that something you can help with?" Aaron asked. Brent nodded and pointed out the correct role name for the training team to Harmony.

"This looks a lot like the same architecture that we use for several other of our applications," Harmony observed. "It's almost like it was copied and pasted from another application."

"That's how we used to do it in the old days," Aaron explained. "You'd look at the reference architecture and just copy that for every application you're setting up. Every Zero Trust environment is tailor-made for each protect surface. Until we know what we need to protect and how it works, we can't tell you what controls should be in there."

"Wearing a one-size-fits-all suit means it's easier to pick your pockets?" Dylan asked.

"It's not the worst analogy I've ever heard," Aaron responded.

"I've heard some companies hire enterprise architects to do this for them?" Nigel asked.

"Enterprise architecture is a key part of an organization's Zero Trust strategy," Aaron confirmed. "They're the group that needs to carry the torch for Zero Trust. They're also the ones that have to do all the care and feeding."

"Cool, so when do we hire these enterprise architects?" Brent asked.

"Oh, I thought you knew." Aaron laughed. "You guys are the enterprise architecture group. Congratulations. There are a lot of ways to do enterprise architecture. But you don't have to hire someone with the title of architect to do it. Having a cross-organizational team helps eliminate silos and provides much-needed perspective."

The team all looked at each other in silence. Brent was the first one to speak up. "I knew I should have asked for a raise."

"The fourth step is to create your Zero Trust policies. I know you're not all firewall administrators, but it's not just about firewall policy. Think about the who, what, where, when, and why. This comes from a Rudyard Kipling poem written in 1902," Aaron said, pointing to the screen:

I have six honest serving men

They taught me all I knew

I call them What and Where and When

And How and Why and Who

"So you are Kipling's six honest serving men. Excuse me, ladies. Three men and three women. All these 'Ws' and 'Hs' are layer seven replacements for an old protocol, source IP, destination IP address, rule set. Here is how I break this down," Aaron said, pointing back to the screen:

Who	What	When	Where	Why	How
User ID	Application ID	Time Limitations	Device ID	Classification	Content ID
Auth type			System Object	Data ID	Threat Protection
			Workload		SSL Decryption
			Geolocation		URL Filtering

John Kindervag's Kipling Method for developing security policies for individual protect surfaces
Courtesy of ON2IT

Aaron's phone rang and he picked it up. He excused himself while the rest of the team reviewed the diagram.

Dylan stood up and walked closer to the screen. "This is different from how I've normally configured policy on a firewall," he observed.

"But we're not just talking about a firewall anymore," Harmony said. "We need to secure a whole protect surface. It would make sense to think of security policy from a larger perspective."

"That makes sense," Dylan agreed. "We need to think about all the controls we'll use at the same time so we can make them work together."

"I don't understand the Why column," Isabelle said.

"I think that's referring to business drivers or regulations," Dylan said. "The 'why' for a policy could be compliance or to achieve a business goal or because it reinforces our Zero Trust strategy. Classification and data ID are about helping classify the data for compliance purposes."

"What about who?" Isabelle asked. "What about the customers?"

"The 'who' is actually why Zero Trust was created," Aaron said, coming back into the room. "We personify computers and computer networks and extend the same trust that we give to an individual to the ones and zeros flowing over a wire. But today, we can build identity into our firewall rules so that while one individual or role or group can get access to a website, other groups are automatically blocked. Similarly, for the 'what' policies, we can write rules based on the Application ID tag of the data that is contained in the payload of the packet. If we were tagging that, we could automate that rule process."

"And then the 'how' statement is, what other things do I need to do to the packet to secure it?" Harmony added. "Do we need to run it through an IPS, or a sandbox, or a URL filter?"

"Exactly," Aaron said. "Kipling would be proud of us. In this case, let's limit the policy on the firewall to just Rose's team and allow only internal access. That's step four, and then step five is to monitor and maintain."

"Does that mean that my team needs to monitor the site? Or does someone else do that part?" Rose asked.

"SharePoint and other services like it are a challenge to secure because it's the users themselves who are allowed to share files with other people," Aaron explained. "For a larger SharePoint site that is hosted online, you should consider looking at a cloud access security broker, or CASB, that has some data leakage protection or DLP capabilities. That's just a fancy way of saying you can use a proxy or endpoint agent to monitor for when people upload files with credit card numbers, for example. But some of those tools will also tell you when a file or folder is shared with the public. In this case, let's just look at who has access manually."

"There are a lot more people who have access to this site than I expected," Rose said. "But it looks like these files are all shared with people inside MarchFit. Is that okay?" she asked.

"I'd say that's up to you," Aaron answered. "This is also a good lesson for us. It's up to the business to decide the answers to many of the questions we'll be asking. Sometimes, we'll need to help educate them about good security practices. But sometimes, they have a business need to share information. For monitor and maintain, we take all of the telemetry—whether it's from a network detection and response tool, or from firewall or server application logs—and then learn from it. As we learn over time, we can make security stronger and stronger."

"This is a perfect place to pause our discussion," Dylan said. "It's actually just about time to join the daily status call with the incident response team. Feel free to stand up and grab some coffee while we get the Zoom meeting set up."

Brent and Nigel stood up and went to the espresso machine, each of them looking at the machine from different angles trying to figure out how to make a cup of coffee. Isabelle demonstrated how the machine worked for them, then took her newly filled cup and went back to the table. Rose excused herself to the washroom just to the side of the entrance of the briefing center. Harmony hunched over her laptop, her face just inches from the screen as she furiously typed an email.

Dylan logged in to their web conferencing tool and displayed it on the video wall, stretching it out along the length of the wall to show all the participants.

Kim and Donna were hunched over speaking with Noor while others filed into the main IT conference room. Kim was wearing a different red suit, but Noor was wearing another black suit and black tie. Peter, the security consultant, was sitting next to Noor, and it looked like he hadn't been to sleep yet and was wearing the same suit from the day before, with more wrinkles. April was also in the room, wearing a yellow track suit, and looked like she had just finished a workout. There were also a number of individuals from across the company logged in remotely.

Noor started speaking, and the conference room camera switched to her. "Thanks to everyone for joining. We've really made a lot of progress . . ." Laughter interrupted her.

"I'm so sorry," said a voice with a heavy Eastern European accent barely containing their laughter, "please continue."

"I'm sorry, who is speaking?" Noor asked. Dylan began scrolling through the long list of participants to see who was talking. His heart dropped when he saw the name "3nc0r3" in the list. Someone clicked the picture of the speaker, and the grainy image of a man in a black hoodie wearing a mask from the band KISS, the one with a star over one eye, took over the whole screen.

"Shut down the conference line," Dylan said urgently, "it's the cybercriminal. He's Zoom-bombing us."

"I wouldn't hang up on me, if I were you. It's very rude," 3nc0r3 said, still laughing. "I've been listening to your conference calls. I know you have decided not to pay my ransom. But this is big-time mistake."

"Don't take it personally," Noor suggested. "It's just business."

"I like America. You do good business. Lots freedom of speeches. You talk so much, but wonder if you want the world to know what you say?"

"What are you talking about?" Noor asked.

"Oh, no," Dylan muttered.

"We have many megabytes of data," 3nc0r3 confirmed. "I know you've been discussing not paying the piper. I will release them to the world if you do not pay the ransom."

Kim leaned over to whisper to Noor, "If that's all he has, then . . ."

"Oh, so sorry," 3nc0r3 corrected. "I meant terabytes. Always get those confused. 753 terabytes. I'll post a sample online now just to show seriousness. Nothing personal, it's just business." He smiled and then dropped from the video conference.

April pulled up her phone and said, "He's already posted the link to download the sample file."

Tweet from the cybercriminal 3nc0r3 sharing a link to sample data online to prove that he had actually stolen MarchFit information

Peter seemed to wake up at that point. "Nobody download that file. I'll grab it and put it through our sandbox to make sure it doesn't have more ransomware."

Key Takeaways

To be successful at anything, and especially in cybersecurity, you need a strategy to achieve your goals. In cybersecurity, the goal is to avoid being breached. Zero Trust is that strategy for success. But what makes a successful strategy? A strategy is a plan to achieve your goals. But you also need to know when you're making progress toward your goals, which is why the best strategies are measurable. There are a number of concepts in cybersecurity that sound like strategies but actually aren't:

- **Defense in depth**—Often, defense in depth is compared to an onion; it has multiple layers. But how many layers do you need before you're secure? In this way, defense in depth fails as a strategy because it's not measurable.
- **Compliance**—Many businesses are required to be in compliance with many different compliance frameworks. Although being compliant may be measurable, the goal isn't to be secure. Compliance is often a minimum starting place that regulators can agree on, but the unique needs of each business require a more tailored approach.
- **Best of breed**—Best of breed versus platform is more of a philosophical debate about the effectiveness of tools. The goal of this approach isn't to prevent a breach; it's to find the best vendors.

The Four Zero Trust Design Principles

The first and most important principle of your Zero Trust strategy is to ensure that you understand how the business makes money and what the organization hopes to achieve. Zero Trust should align with business outcomes, not prevent the business from operating effectively. There are a huge number of tools or products available to help you along in your Zero Trust journey, but it's important to always keep these four principles in mind to stay focused on the big picture:

1. Focus on business outcomes.
2. Design from the inside out.
3. Determine who/what needs access.
4. Inspect and log all traffic.

The Five-Step Zero Trust Design Methodology

To make your Zero Trust journey achievable, you need a repeatable process to follow. The first step is to break down your environment into smaller pieces that you need to protect. Many organizations focus on reducing the scope of their attack surface. An attack surface is all the possible points of attack a threat actor could leverage to access a system and steal or exfiltrate data. In practice, the attack surface for a global organization with users working remotely could encompass the whole world. Rather than focusing on your "attack surface," which is huge and hard for you to control, the Zero Trust design methodology focuses on what you can control: protect surfaces. Each protect surface helps you limit the blast radius of any attack to just that portion of your environment by doing the following five steps:

- Define the protect surface.
- Map the transaction flows.
- Architect a Zero Trust environment.
- Create Zero Trust policies.
- Monitor and maintain.

The Zero Trust Implementation Curve

When beginning your Zero Trust journey, you'll need to start by going through the five-step methodology on non-business-critical systems. You want to create an environment for learning where making a mistake won't impact your organization. If you already have a Business Continuity Plan (BCP) or a Business Impact Assessment (BIA), these documents should have already categorized the applications that are most important to your business. Once you are ready to begin working on critical protect surfaces, you should focus on the most important systems first to protect your crown jewels as quickly as possible:

- Learning protect surfaces
- Practice protect surfaces
- The "crown jewels" (aka business-critical protect surfaces)
- Secondary protect surfaces
- Tertiary protect surfaces

Chapter 3
Trust Is a Vulnerability

As Dylan was walking into the MarchFit offices, his cell phone rang. It was an automated recording from his pharmacy, so he put the phone up to his ear and listened. Ahead of him a man held the door open to the South MarchFit corridors for a woman carrying a potted plant. As Dylan walked past the security desk, he could see two monitors displaying sixteen cameras each, but the pictures were too small for him to be able to tell what was going on in the images. The security guard was speaking with a woman at the other side of the desk, not looking at the cameras or the entrance or Dylan. Dylan continued to walk toward the entrance when another security guard walked through the door. Dylan followed him in without swiping his badge, which he realized was still in his pocket. He wasn't even displaying his ID like he was supposed to at all times while he was in the building.

Inside the security door was a vestibule for the elevators. The security guard got into one of the elevators and held the door open for Dylan, but Dylan waved him off, pointing to his cell phone. The guard nodded and the elevator doors closed. On the opposite side of the room, there was another card swipe on the door leading into the secure office space beyond. This door was propped open and Dylan could see a water delivery man rolling a cart full of bottled water down one of the aisles. Dylan walked through this door as well.

Dylan knew his way around the offices by this point, but he hadn't been at the company long enough for most people to recognize him. He wondered how far he could make it inside the office before someone stopped him. Would anyone stop him? He pressed the end button on the call—the recording had already repeated twice—and continued walking.

With the phone still against his ear, Dylan walked around looking at the hallways as though it were his first time there. He noted the locations of the cameras embedded in the ceiling. Although he couldn't tell which direction they were facing, there seemed to be paths he could take where he wouldn't be seen. He walked past a room that had several printers with office supplies lining the walls. There was a stack of printed documents waiting to be picked up. There was a recycling bin full of documents next to the printer. Dylan couldn't read them as he walked past, but this made him wonder if there were any locked shred bins where sensitive documents could be placed. He didn't notice any as he continued his unsupervised tour.

He walked down one hallway closer to the R&D labs where either side of the hallway was lined with six-foot-tall filing cabinets. The keys to each of the filing cabinets were conveniently located inside the locks at the top center of each cabinet. Dylan realized that if he locked the locks and walked away with the keys, he'd be doing a kind of analog version of ransomware.

At the end of the hallway was a glass door with the red light of a card reader flashing. A dull hum was reverberating from the air conditioning behind the walls, and he realized that this was probably the door to the MarchFit data center.

An engineer walked out, and Dylan trotted quickly toward the door. The man actually stopped and held the door open for Dylan before it could close. Still on the phone, Dylan nodded to the man, and he continued down the hallway.

Dylan was greeted by the arctic air coming out of the data center room. He let the door close behind him and took the room in. It was probably around a thousand square feet—not the biggest data center he'd ever been in, but then most of MarchFit's operations were done in the cloud. There were several rows of cabinets full of the flashing lights of servers, storage, firewalls, routers, and switches. Many of the cabinet doors were slightly ajar. There was a plastic cart sitting next to the door and Dylan briefly contemplated removing one of the servers and walking out just to see how long it might take for someone to notice.

A server admin walked around the corner and almost bumped into Dylan. "Oh, excuse me," the man said. "Were you looking for someone?"

"I was supposed to meet Noor here, but I'm a little early," Dylan lied. "I'll just meet her in her office," he said, and walked out of the data center.

Dylan walked into the briefing center to find that the team had started their meeting without him. Aaron was reviewing the five design principles with the team and had displayed the principles on the video wall:

1. Define the protect surface.
2. Map the transaction flows.

3. Architect a Zero Trust environment.
4. Create Zero Trust policies.
5. Monitor and maintain.

"We've gotten through a few practice protect surfaces, but I think now it's time to move on to a learning protect surface. We'll need a protect surface with a little more complexity. Anyone have a suggestion?" Aaron said.

"How about we look at our physical security," Dylan said, sitting down and opening his laptop.

"I think that's an excellent choice," Aaron said.

"I thought we wanted to work on systems that didn't matter if we break them," Brent said. "Wouldn't people get really mad if we locked everyone out?"

"Actually," Harmony said, "the card readers are designed to work when the network is down or even in a power outage. I think the card readers have a local database, so they'll remember the permissions of people who had gone through the doors recently. Worst case, we can just prop the doors open like we did during the incident."

Dylan began to explain his experiment with physical security earlier in the morning.

"That's brilliant," Nigel said. "I didn't know you were so sneaky."

"That's just it—I'm not. I was just distracted," Dylan admitted.

"Physical security is the perfect analogy for Zero Trust," Aaron said. "It's easier to talk about since we're not talking about imaginary invisible things. And I think people instinctively understand security. Security is a part of why we come together as a social animal: We come together for mutual protection. As much as we talk about how Zero Trust does away with the perimeter, it's still important for us to have a foundation to talk about. So my first question for the group is where does physical security start?"

"Is it the doors to the building?" Brent asked.

"What about the fence around the property?" Rose asked.

"Or the camera system?" Harmony offered.

"What about the security guards?" Nigel asked. "Anyone could hop the fence if there weren't guards behind it."

"You guys are all talking about elements of perimeter security. That makes sense in the physical world where a human has to go through the perimeter to get inside a building. But that's not the way things work in cyberspace. Ask yourself what would happen if someone invented a teleporter like in *Star Trek*. Those perimeter controls would still be important, but you'd need to shift the way you thought about security. The answer to this in Zero Trust is the protect surface."

"What does that mean? How do we change the perimeter?" Brent asked.

"That's the question we need to ask for every protect surface. So for physical security, we need to understand what it is that we're protecting. Is it the life safety of the people in the building? Is it the servers in the data center? Is it the computers? Or the paper documents?"

"Isn't it all of the above?" Dylan asked.

"Yes and no," Aaron answered. "Again, physical security gives us another great analogy for Zero Trust. Inside the building, we create different areas where we allow anyone to roam freely. If you get access to the office areas, you can go to any one of the many cubicles. That's an example of containment. If something bad were to happen, we have contained the blast radius of that damage to one area, but hopefully other areas are still safe. In this example, we place the controls adjacent to the things that we are protecting. We put cameras and fire suppression and card access around the data center, but maybe we don't need all of those things at the perimeter of the facility in the parking lots. But that's exactly what we're doing in cybersecurity when we put a firewall by the Internet and call it a day."

"Doesn't that just mean we need better firewalls?" Brent asked.

"Unfortunately, there's this secondary attack surface. It's called the internal network." Aaron laughed at his own joke then continued. "When we research incidents, there's this concept called dwell time. We want to know how long the threat actor was in your network before they were discovered. When you haven't done any containment, the dwell times will be very long. Sometimes cybercriminals have been reported to have been inside a network for six months or a year before they are detected. For MarchFit's physical security, you do have different areas and security checkpoints. Dylan was noticed pretty quickly once he reached the data center, but he could have spent a lot of time in the office areas before he was noticed."

Harmony folded her arms and leaned back in her chair. "So if I'm understanding you correctly, the idea with Zero Trust is that we move the controls away from the perimeter to the smaller protect surfaces. And that allows us to use much more granular controls that are specific to each protect surface?"

"Well said, Harmony," Aaron said. "And those smaller protect surfaces allow us to change our policies more rapidly. If you had the president come for a visit, you might restrict access to certain areas where employees might normally be able to go, for example. We still have monitoring via closed-circuit television cameras that monitor the perimeter so we can alert on when things come in and out of the building, just like we want to log all of the traffic coming through our firewalls."

"But what about the air ducts, like in *Die Hard*?" Brent asked.

"It turns out that we have a great physical security resource already onsite," Aaron continued, ignoring Brent's question. "Let me ask Noor if we can borrow him." Aaron typed a message into his phone. Several minutes later, Peter Liu knocked on the door to the executive briefing center (EBC) and walked in.

"You guys needed me?" Peter asked.

"Peter, nice to see you again," Dylan said. "How's the recovery effort going?"

"We opened the file that 3nc0r3 released in a sandbox, and it looked clean. Noor and her team are reviewing the data to see if it's legit and hopefully will find where it came from," Peter said. "But I thought you guys had a question about Zero Trust? I'm not sure if I'm going to be much help."

"I wanted to see if we could pick your brain for a bit about physical security," Aaron explained. "You guys know that Peter is the lead security consultant helping with our incident response, but I knew him at a previous company where he got his start as a penetration tester. He had a real knack for breaking into some of the most secure facilities in the world."

Peter shrugged. "What happens in Vegas stays in Vegas."

"Let's talk about the transaction flow for what happens when you swipe your card," Aaron said. "How would you take advantage of the trust relationships in the card reader system to get into a building?"

Peter looked thoughtful for a moment, then held up his visitor card. "March-Fit uses a proximity card system. I've not looked at what you guys are doing, but assuming the cards aren't encrypted, you can buy a cheap RFID cloner on Amazon. I'd just clone the badge of someone with access and I'd be in."

"What? Really?" Isabelle asked.

"Assume for a moment that the badges are encrypted. What trust relationships would you look to exploit then?" Aaron asked.

"There are still some ways to get around encryption," Peter said. "If I were a nation-state, I might hack the card reader company."

"How would that help?" Brent asked.

"Most card reader companies use the same encryption key for all their clients. You have to ask very nicely with a cherry on top to get your own unique encryption key," Peter explained. "So if you're wearing a tinfoil hat, you can expect a CIA agent to go wherever they want. But short of that, I'd want to look at the card readers themselves."

"You can hack our card readers?" Harmony asked.

"That wouldn't be my first choice," Peter laughed. "Depending on the card reader, I'd have a couple of options. Given the age of the building, I'd expect that these card readers aren't on the network. Older card readers are usually wired back to a control panel, and for the most part older card readers use a protocol called Wiegand, which was created back in the 1980s. There are YouTube tutorials about how to fit a small tap behind the card reader to collect all the unencrypted card credentials, and you can use that to get access."

"There's no way to encrypt that data?" Dylan asked.

"There's a newer protocol called Open Supervised Device Protocol, or OSDP, that supports encryption, but not every card reader supports it. You'd have the same issue if the card readers were on wireless or wired network connections. You still have to enable encryption. Often I find that most of the physical security integrators that install the card readers don't configure them securely. They're just there to do the install as quickly as possible. And they don't want to come back, so they'll also configure those systems for remote access. So I'd look to see if I could find a way just to get in remotely and give myself all the access I want."

"You've really done all that?" Harmony asked with a hint of envy in her voice.

"It's all about finding the easiest way in. If I can get a job as a cleaning person or pretend to be one, there might not be much technical acumen needed. Let's take a field trip," Peter said, standing up and moving toward the door.

The group followed him down the stairs to the security desk in the main lobby. There were two computers. One was running the card reader system and was configured to print visitor badges. The other had dual monitors displaying a number of small CCTV streams. The security guard initially walked over to the group and asked, "Can I help you?"

"Can we talk to the person who runs the security computers?" Peter asked. Nodding, the security guard at the desk picked up his radio and said something into it. While he was talking, Harmony sat down at the computer and started clicking.

Before the security guard could say anything, Harmony exclaimed, "This computer is running Windows 7?"

"How long has that OS been end-of-lifed?" Brent asked.

"I don't understand. Our support team completed the Windows 10 upgrade project a couple years ago," Isabelle said.

"These computers probably aren't on the domain. They're supplied by the security installer," Peter said. "This is pretty common, unfortunately."

"But they're on our network," Harmony confirmed by running the ipconfig -all command from the command prompt. "These PCs are on the same network as the rest of the workstations." Then she ran the netstat command. "Wait, is this desktop also the server running the card access software? It's connecting to a bunch of local devices also on the user subnets. We put the card readers on the same network as everyone else?" Harmony asked, shocked.

Unfortunately, Peter said, "if there's not an infrastructure team that knows that they can push back and design the network with Zero Trust in mind, your physical security integrator will do what they can to get the computer up and running."

"Let's talk about process," Aaron said, turning to the security guard manager who had come out of his office on the inside of north MarchFit. The guard was several inches taller than Dylan and was wearing a dark blue uniform with the security company logo embroidered on his sleeves. His badge read "Glenn."

"When a new employee starts, how do you get their badge ready?" Aaron asked.

"We'll get an email on Friday letting us know a new employee will start on Monday," Glenn answered, folding his arms. "We ask for ID when they show up, of course. Then we take their picture."

"How do you know what parts of the building they need access to?" Peter asked.

"We just give them the basics unless HR says they need to get into other places. We just hit this drop-down menu here," he said, pointing to the screen, "and we pick the door groups they need."

"Can anyone just sit down at the desk and start typing?" Dylan asked.

"There's always someone sitting at the desk," Glenn said defensively.

Dylan remembered his first day where there was no one at the desk but chose not to say anything. Instead, he asked, "When you change shifts, do you have to log out of the computer and the new guard logs in?"

"Oh, no. That's way too complicated for the crew. Not all my crew knows how to open the camera or card reader windows. Just too technical for some," Glenn explained. "We have to keep the windows up or else things get really confusing during shift changes."

"What happens if something breaks?" Dylan asked. Aaron nodded as Dylan asked the question, like he was about to ask the same thing.

"Oh, we have the number of the company that manages the card access system. They have some people that can get in remotely to get everything working again. They're really fast," Glenn said.

Harmony sat down at the desk and started looking at the computer. After a few seconds, she said, "Oh crud. They've installed their own remote access software."

"Why is that bad?" Rose asked.

"It's really easy for bad guys to get in using that software. We should probably shut that down. Right, Aaron? Dylan?" she said, looking to the two of them.

Aaron nodded but held up his finger. "Just a few more questions before we get to the architecture conversation," Aaron said. "What do you do for visitors?"

"Oh, you should know that since you're wearing a visitor badge." Glenn pointed out the visitor tag Aaron was wearing.

"Let's explain the process for the folks who don't know," Aaron said.

"It's just like the process for giving employees badges, except it's temporary and the cards are reused. We have to have a regular employee sponsor them and supervise them while they're in the building. We make a copy of their driver's license so we have it on file if we find out something happened later," Glenn said.

"Do you have any problems with the cameras?" Dylan asked, pointing at the other monitors where the cameras were being displayed.

"Oh yeah. All the time," Glenn said. "We have to get a ladder to reboot some of the cameras when they freeze up."

"How often do they freeze?" Dylan asked.

"The bad cameras? At least once a week. But you never know which ones are bad. We have to watch the guards on patrol and check in with the radios to see if the image has frozen. I usually have the night shift do that. But sometimes we go back and find that the recordings are missing too. When it happened the first time, I thought it was that hacker, but it turned out the disk was full."

Harmony pulled out her laptop and began typing at a command prompt. Then she pulled up a web browser and after a few clicks, the camera facing the security guard desk was showing video on her screen. "The cameras are also on the network," she said. "I took a wild guess, and the password for the cameras is MarchFit."

"I think you'll find other building automation systems or air conditioning have similar configurations. The contractors come in and their only requirement is that they get the system working. There isn't any accountability to them if the system isn't secure. The organization needs to provide this through contracts and oversight," Peter explained.

"This is one of the first lessons we need to take to heart when it comes to Zero Trust," Aaron said. "When we think about transaction flows, we're not just talking about how packets get from point A to point B. We also need to think about the business processes and relationships to give us the big picture. Let's head back to the EBC to think about what controls we put in place to address the problems we've discovered."

The group walked back upstairs, but Peter paused at the entrance and stopped them from going in. "I've got one last thing to show you. When we exited the EBC, there was a motion sensor placed above the door that automatically unlocked it. That makes it more convenient than having to press a button to get out, but there's a problem with that." Peter pointed up through the glass, and they could see the green light on the sensor. Peter began folding a piece of paper he had in his pocket into a paper airplane. He slid it between the small gap where the glass of the door met the glass of the wall of the EBC, then lightly tossed it into the room. It glided a few feet before landing, but that was just enough to trigger the motion sensor. Peter opened the door without swiping his badge, then bowed like a magician as he held the door open for the team.

Once everyone was sitting back in the EBC, Aaron pulled up a web browser on the video wall and went to a website called Shodan.io. He searched for the IP addresses that they saw on the guard's computer, and a huge list of devices was displayed. Aaron clicked on one of the IP addresses, and it showed a lot of detail about the device. "There's a lot of information freely available on the Internet about the devices MarchFit has on its network. It sounds like Harmony had some ideas on what we can do to improve our architecture. Harmony?"

"The first thing I'd want to do is to move all the cameras and card readers onto private addresses. I also don't think the cameras or the card readers need to be on the same network as other devices. We can put them all on separate non-routed networks so no one can get to them."

"That's a great use of microsegmentation," Aaron agreed.

"What's that?" Isabelle asked, turning her chair to face Aaron.

"You've heard the phrase 'never put your eggs in one basket'?" Aaron asked. She nodded and he continued, "Microsegmentation just means we're putting different kinds of eggs in different baskets to keep them separate. What else would you guys want to do?" he asked, looking around the room

"Maybe have different passwords for each camera," Rose suggested.

"That's a good suggestion," Aaron said, "but we also want to consider the complexity of managing all those different passwords. Do the guards need a password vault? Can the camera management company manage that? That's a good transition to creating Zero Trust policies. MarchFit has some good policies in place for sponsoring visitors. And generally speaking we expect people to wear the badges in a visible place. What suggestions do you have for other areas?"

"Maybe we should have the guards have separate logins to the camera and card reader system in case someone walks up while they're distracted," Dylan suggested.

"Can we put up posters reminding people not to tailgate?" Rose asked.

"Excellent suggestion," Aaron said.

"We definitely need a better process for having the management company get remote access into those systems," Harmony said. "Brent, can we get a sponsored account for them? They can at least use VPN to get in. And for goodness' sake, we should be running a current operating system."

"What about the time of day?" Nigel asked.

"It's not even close to lunchtime," Brent answered.

"No, mate," Nigel corrected. "Can we change the access policies based on the time of day? Maybe some people don't need access after hours or on weekends. That's policy, right?"

"Right you are," Aaron confirmed. "And when we talk about monitoring, we might consider additional alerting if someone unexpectedly comes in during one of those times."

"For the monitor and maintain phase," Dylan began, "if we had guards using unique logins, we'd have better audit trails when something changed."

"That's definitely a best practice," Peter added. "I'd also suggest sending physical security logs to the SIEM. You can use card swipes as behavioral triggers to help make determinations based on whether employees are in the office or working from home."

"Is there a way to integrate the camera system with the card reader system?" Rose asked.

"That's a great idea," Peter said.

"Why would we want to do that?" Brent asked.

"I've seen it done before," Peter said. "When someone swipes their card, their picture pops up on the video screen so the guard can verify that it really is the person in the video. Not every video system is compatible, so we'd have to check to see if there's an API between the two systems."

"I've got an idea," Isabelle said. "Can we send emails to sponsors when visitors go through doors? That might be helpful if someone wanders away."

"That's a wonderful suggestion," Aaron confirmed. "I'd also suggest that we have the card reader system produce daily or weekly reports to send to staff who are responsible for certain areas like the data center. But you guys missed one of the biggest issues."

The group was silent for an uncomfortable period of time. Dylan finally broke the silence. "What did we miss? I can't think of anything."

"The security guards have a problem with several cameras that aren't working correctly. They have a process for incident response when they see an issue happening. It's good that they are able to reboot them, but with Zero Trust, we need to get to the root cause of an issue to proactively prevent the problem from happening again," Aaron replied.

Key Takeaways

You can't have cybersecurity without physical security. If a threat actor can walk into your data center, it's game over. With today's card readers and video surveillance systems, however, you can't have physical security without cybersecurity.

Cybersecurity controls for physical security systems are often overlooked. Often, these controls are installed by third-party integrators as a part of a new building construction or when a company moves into a commercial real estate space. Many times, a different third-party security guard company will be in charge of using that system day to day. When so many different groups are involved with a system, it's often difficult to secure because no one group is responsible for the security of that system. A big part of identifying a protect surface is understanding who has responsibility for that system.

You don't need to know how to pick a lock to get access to a secure facility. As mentioned in this chapter, some penetration testers will clone a badge using an inexpensive RFID cloner. Sometimes there are even easier ways like sliding a piece of paper under a door to trigger a motion sensor that automatically unlocks a door as a convenience to employees. Sometimes the building HVAC system creates too much air pressure in a room and doors don't close properly. And sometimes, employees prop doors open for convenience.

Physical security is the perfect analogy for Zero Trust. When designing physical security controls, we naturally place controls around the things we're trying to protect. When organizations perform physical penetration testing, they are often surprised to discover the simple methods that criminals can use to get complete access to a facility. But because of the fault tolerance built into these systems, they can be a part of a learning protect surface without concerns about taking the whole system down.

Several different transaction flows need to be mapped as a part of the card reader process. First, the process for a card reader processing a card swipe. Then there is the process for assigning credentials. Finally, there should be a separate process to help visitors get temporary access to company facilities. This chapter focused on the transaction flow mapping portion of the Zero Trust design methodology, and it's important to note that there can be multiple transaction flows within a single protect surface. Some protect surfaces may include multiple applications, as the example in this chapter did with both card access and closed-circuit television (CCTV).

Many organizations today employ proximity badges for employees so that they can just tap their badge on a reader rather than use a magnetic card swipe, although magnetic stripe readers are also still in use today. The identification information on a magnetic stripe card can be easily read so long as the card is swiped, so a threat actor needs to have physical possession to make a copy. However, RFID cards can be copied at a distance, exposing the credential, unless the cards are encrypted. While some proximity cards may be encrypted, there are ways of getting around that. Card production companies may use a single encryption key for all their cards, for example. Often the card readers are connected to a control panel and many card readers aren't configured to use encrypted communications between the card reader and panel, so a criminal could place a tap behind the card reader to steal user credentials for later access. Other card readers use Ethernet or wireless communication, and these channels also need to require encrypted communication.

Often card readers and cameras are placed on public networks that can be reached by other devices both inside and outside an organization. Search engines like Shodan allow easy scans of vulnerable IoT devices like cameras that are exposed to the Internet, and devices like this are routinely compromised as an entry point into corporate networks. For this reason, card readers and cameras are both good candidates for a Zero Trust concept called microsegmentation.

In many corporate networks, all networked devices—including computers, printers, card readers, cameras, air conditioning systems, etc.—are placed on the same network or virtual local area network (VLAN). In this standard configuration, a computer can communicate with a printer, but it can also connect to a video camera or be used to take over the air conditioning system. In other words, by placing all of the devices on the same VLAN, we are saying that we trust all of these devices to communicate with one another.

Microsegmentation creates smaller VLANs or zones where only devices that need to communicate with one another are allowed to be located in the same zone. Employee computers are placed in one zone, whereas printers are placed in another zone and only the network traffic that we expect to be sent to a printer is allowed. For physical security, only devices that have a need to connect to card readers or cameras should have access—usually the card access servers or the video archive servers. Because the security guard's workstation is not a trusted device, it is not allowed to talk directly to the camera network. Instead, it should communicate with a hardened intermediary server designed to allow access to only the cameras the guard has been authorized to view.

The security guard mentioned experiencing issues with the system and sometimes ignoring those alarms. They know how to fix the issue when a camera freezes, but they never addressed the root cause of the problem.

There's a big difference between incident management and problem management. Incident management is all about the processes you use to respond to incidents in real time. Cybersecurity teams are often built around having mature incident response processes and plans to be prepared when bad things happen. Problem management is focused on finding the root cause of why whole categories of incidents occur and preventing them from happening. If an organization focuses exclusively on incident management without addressing the underlying source of the issues, the risk is that they'll be stuck in firefighting mode. A team can become desensitized to alarms and bad things can slip through. The reason that Zero Trust is successful is that it addresses the underlying source of incidents—trust. Zero Trust attempts to help prevent or contain future incidents through problem management.

Chapter 4
The Crown Jewels

Dylan knocked on the slightly open door to Donna's office. "Is this still a good time to talk?" he asked. Donna was wearing a large pair of noise-canceling headphones and typing on a large manual calculator that printed numbers on a receipt as she typed. Dylan took two steps in and waved to get her attention.

"Dylan? Hello," Donna said, peering over papers arranged neatly into stacks that reminded Dylan of a 3D rendering of a map of downtown. She took off the headphones and said, "Perfect timing, I was just finishing up. Please have a seat." A small circular table near the entrance was covered with stacks of binders. The topmost binder read "2021 Audit Report."

"How is Project Zero Trust going?" she asked.

"It's been a couple weeks, but we're starting to make progress. But the consultant kicked me out and said I needed to go figure out how the business makes money. Isabelle suggested I should start with you," Dylan said as he sat down in the chair next to the circular table.

"That's quite the consultant you've got there. What do you want to know?" Donna asked.

"I know we have pretty good margins on each TreadMarch. Then there are the work-appropriate workout clothes. The monthly subscription is another big part of that. Zero Trust needs to be able to protect and enable the business at the same time," Dylan explained.

"What about that hacker?" Donna asked as she walked around the desk to sit in the chair next to Dylan.

"Unfortunately, the data he released was real. Thankfully, it was just a bunch of old telemetry from the treadmills that was being stored in the cloud, so there wasn't any personal information in it. I think it underscores how important the work we're doing is right now," Dylan said as he opened his notebook to an empty page and wrote the date at the top.

"What questions did you have, then?" Donna asked.

"What are your biggest priorities right now as CFO?" Dylan asked.

"There are several key areas that we'll be focusing on this year. We need to ensure that we have the financial data to enable our leadership to make the best strategic decisions," Donna explained. "The pandemic has massively increased our profitability as people aren't going to gyms, but we don't expect that to last forever. At the same time, we're preparing for our new product launch, which we expect to take the company in a whole new direction. To be able to navigate that, we've got to have the right insights to be able to respond to our existing consumers and new consumers so that we're investing in the right areas at the right time."

"I think it's really cool that you're making data-driven decisions," Dylan said. "Do you have enough support to be able to make the insights you need?"

"Oh, numbers always have a story to tell. You just have to listen to them. I guess you're looking into the Ides?" Donna asked.

"The Ides?" Dylan asked.

"Oh, you hadn't heard it called that yet?" Donna said apologetically. "It's what most people call our ERP system. It's lovingly referred as the Ides of March. That's when Julius Caesar was killed, but there was this witch who told Caesar to beware the Ides of March. So. Beware."

"Have there been issues with the Ides?" Dylan asked.

"Nothing specific. It's just incredibly complicated, and I don't think anyone knows how it works. They did a lot with security a few years ago for credit cards. Now our stores use end-to-end encryption, which means that the credit card number is encrypted at the card reader itself and isn't unencrypted until it reaches the payment processor. This has greatly reduced our costs when it comes to credit card compliance because of how much simpler our controls are. That's an example of Zero Trust, right? Not trusting the devices or the network reduced our costs. I just signed our latest PCI compliance report, if you want to see that. I'm sure I can find it here somewhere." She stood up and began looking through the different stacks of binders on the table. Seconds later a binder labeled *PCI assessment results* was in Dylan's hands.

"I'll check that out," Dylan said, putting the binder into his backpack. "I was actually hoping this would just be the start of a conversation. I've always thought that finance was just another part of the security team. You help create the budgets, but you also prevent fraud. We need your expertise in helping make sure a breach never happens to us again. What are the biggest concerns you have right now?"

"What about how money leaves the organization?" Donna said. "Isn't that how all those business email compromise things happen?"

"Exactly. Let's say I've got a new vendor, like this consultant. How would you find out about it to know who to pay and how much?" Dylan asked.

"That's easy. One of my team would enter the vendor into Ides. Then we'd attach an invoice and cut a check."

"Who has access to create a new vendor or to write a check?"

"Everyone on my team," she said, but then hesitated. "I don't know if anyone outside my team has access. I used to get reports on this at my last job. Is that something we can set up?"

"You bet. What about reports of all new vendors that get created? Or all invoices?"

"That would be amazing," Donna said. "I thought we'd need to buy some new software to be able to do that. I've always wished we could have multiple approvals for invoices. Is that something we can do as well?"

"We definitely need to do that! I always like to think about processes before technology," Dylan said. "We're always focused on getting shiny new technology to solve our problems. But the biggest frustration from people is always that they need to do something to get their job done and the technology makes it harder."

"Process before technology. Can I steal that?" Donna asked.

"Of course," Dylan laughed.

"It's funny. I think we're both doing the same thing," Donna observed. "I need Ides to understand how the business operates in real time to protect the business from going the wrong direction, and you need to understand how the business operates in order to protect Ides. There's a nice symmetry there, don't you think?"

Dylan walked into the MarchFit lobby buzzing. He noticed MarchFit's slogan engraved into the wall above the entrance to the building: "Every Step Matters." As he walked up the stairs to the conference room, Dylan thought about all the steps he had taken on his treadmill at home. He thought about all the outdoor walks he had taken while on conference calls over the last two years. It didn't feel like a particular step made much difference at the time. But each step made the one after that possible.

He paused outside the door to the conference room. Aaron was at the video wall explaining something, but Dylan couldn't hear what it was. He watched as the team interacted, each feeding off the energy of the person before them.

Harmony was standing, gesturing animatedly toward Aaron. Dylan pulled the door open slightly so he could hear them speak. "I keep hearing security experts talk about how we should just be doing the basics, but they never really say what the basics are beyond patching and MFA. Isn't that what we're doing with Zero Trust?" she asked. Dylan smiled seeing the team really get engaged.

"Part of the problem with just saying to follow best practices is that everyone's environment is so different," Aaron explained. "It's great to follow best practices, but there are actually a lot of different ways that you can accomplish implementing them—and how you implement them and what you implement them on takes a lot of specific knowledge about the environment. As a strategy, Zero Trust helps focus your efforts toward the most effective ways of securing your organization. This is why mapping the transaction flows is one of the first things that you need to do."

"We're ready to start the first major protect surface," Aaron said as Dylan walked in. "Your business continuity plan has several high-priority applications that you need to secure, but I think we're ready to start work on our ERP system. We've focused primarily on network-based controls in the applications we've looked at before, but to implement Zero Trust in the ERP, we'll need to dive a little deeper into the application."

"We call it Ides," Dylan said. Brent and Nigel both smirked at this.

"It sounds like you're ready to beware of the Ides of March?" Aaron said. "I take it your conversations with your stakeholders are going well, then. Did you learn anything about the ERP system?"

"It seems like there are a lot more ways that we can lose money than we can make it," Dylan said, defeated.

"Dylan, you're not just learning the business outcomes," Aaron encouraged. "You're creating the relationships and trust that you'll need to help sustain the changes that we're making. We need to align security with the business, and you can't do that tucked away in a conference room or a data center. The people in the business are the business, and you have to align with them."

"That helps, but the ERP system is huge and incredibly complex," Dylan said. "But we'll give it a try."

"No!" Aaron said. "Try not. Do. Or do not. There is no try." The table erupted with howls of laughter at this. "Sorry, I've always wanted to say that," Aaron responded between laughs.

"Where should we begin?" Rose asked.

"I'm glad you asked, Rose." Aaron was serious again. "I apologize for not telling you this sooner, but when we began, I asked for a security consultant to come in and perform an assessment. And she's ready to give us her report." With a few clicks, a Zoom window appeared on the video wall and a woman appeared on the screen. "This is Peng. We've worked together on several projects and she's an ERP security specialist. What have you found, Peng?"

"Let's start with the good news." Peng shared her screen showing the text of the report. "We saw that there were a number of good security practices already in place with your ERP system. One of the first things we look at is the default usernames for the application itself. Those had been changed. It looks like many of those defaults had been changed to be references to Julius Caesar."

"That makes sense." Harmony chuckled.

"Also, the ERP system has been configured to encrypt all traffic by default, including the backend connections to the database. And the databases themselves are encrypted as well so that even if the servers running the database are compromised, an attacker wouldn't be able to get access to the data. Although database encryption isn't required, there are state privacy statutes that indicate if the data is encrypted and you experience a compromise, you don't have to do a breach notification."

"This is going to be easier than I thought," Brent said.

"Unfortunately," Peng interrupted, "that's all the good news."

Nigel crumpled up a piece of paper and threw it at Brent. "Stop jinxing us, mate!"

"The bad news," Peng began, "is that the ERP system itself hasn't been patched in about five years. This means it doesn't have the latest software updates, new security features, et cetera."

"That makes sense," Rose said. "The company was started about five years ago."

"So it's never actually been patched since we started?" Dylan asked.

"This is actually a very common scenario," Peng said. "Usually it happens for a number of reasons. Maybe the team is understaffed and has to prioritize meeting project deadlines. It could be because the ERP team doesn't have the organizational support to accommodate any downtime. You're actually in better shape than most other ERP implementations, which haven't been patched in ten years."

"That doesn't make me feel any better," Dylan said.

"Let's keep going. Peng, can you tell us about how the transactions flow through the ERP system?" Aaron asked.

"Sure. Let me start with the 10,000-foot overview. ERP systems don't come out of the box ready to support your business. There are a lot of different modules you can choose from. And most businesses customize all these different parts of the application to suit their business with specialized developers. Developers work on their code in a development environment, which is usually an exact copy of the main production system so that they can make sure their code works. Then the code is migrated to a test environment, and if it works there after some review, it is then migrated into production. From a process perspective, MarchFit does have the appropriate separation of duties so that developers can't migrate code into production by themselves; they have to rely on others to do this work for them."

"That's good. What issues did you find?" Aaron asked.

"One challenge we noted is that MarchFit uses real data in dev and test. So the developers have access to real personal data. There are tools available to mask that data or to use dummy data instead. We highly recommend this."

"Is that it?" Brent asked. "That seems pretty minor."

"Have you ever seen *Superman III*?" Peng asked, not waiting for an answer. "Your ERP system uses a specialized code language that isn't supported by most commercial code scanning tools. This means that even though you have good separation-of-duties processes, and even if you're running vulnerability scans, you wouldn't be able to detect Richard Pryor injecting code that steals pennies from every transaction, for example."

"Is Richard Pryor one of our developers?" Harmony whispered to Rose. Rose shook her head silently.

"Even though you removed the default naming conventions, there were a large number of people with superuser status on the ERP system itself, which is a concern. And when we looked further into the code, there were hard-coded passwords inside the code. We also saw that a former developer had created a finance report in production that was still being sent to his Gmail address. Although there is extensive user acceptance testing during deployments, this is all being done in the code without oversight. So, in short, the internals of an ERP system are usually a blind spot for security teams."

"We also know that although MarchFit has a vulnerability management program and does regular scans, they don't scan inside the ERP system," Aaron explained.

"Oh, Richard Pryor was a comedian!" Harmony exclaimed, looking up from her computer. She looked up and realized she had said it out loud. "Sorry!"

"Oh no, he's great," Peng said. "You should definitely check him out."

"So what kinds of things could go wrong with these issues?" Dylan asked.

"From a vulnerability perspective, we should be concerned that a disgruntled developer with superuser access could create a fake company, then create a fake invoice, and have payments sent directly to that account. Or a malicious actor could inject a bit of code to ship new treadmills to random addresses all over the world instead of where they're supposed to go."

"A hacker could really do all that?" Rose asked.

"I've detailed the transaction flows in my report," Peng said. "For each transaction, we walk through both the business use cases, but we also walk through how each transaction could be used against the business. We call that a 'misuse case.' We've provided a prioritized list of each of the misuse cases, but the ones we've already gone through are the major ones that there weren't any compensating controls to prevent or even detect."

"Thank you, Peng. Very helpful," Aaron said. "She's already sent us a copy of her report, which details all of the transaction flows for the second step in the Zero Trust methodology. As we move on to the third step, architecting the Zero Trust environment, we'll be doing something a little different."

"That's sounds scary, considering this is such an important system," Dylan said.

"Most of the time, we don't need new tools to implement Zero Trust for a particular protect surface," Aaron said. "Zero Trust isn't any one tool. But in this case, we are missing a key tool in our toolkit. Imagine a general commanding an army. They'd have soldiers, artillery, radios, and maybe even tanks. They could develop a strategy with the tools they had at hand. But imagine that general didn't have any fighter jets. That would be a pretty big gap in their capabilities that would be difficult to overcome no matter how good their strategy was."

"So we need a new tool?" Isabelle asked.

"In this case, yes," Aaron answered. "There is a specialized tool I had in mind to help address the gaps around the ERP system, Ides. Here are the gaps that Peng identified in her report." With a flourish, Aaron waved his hand and displayed the report on the wall monitor and the following bullets appeared:

- Specialized programming languages are not supported by most security code review tools.
- ERP change control is often a manual process and isn't built into the ERP system itself.
- Traditional vulnerability management tools don't scan applications or code updates.

- Compliance-management mechanisms, like enforcing password standards, configurations, or access to sensitive data, aren't native to ERP systems.
- Application logs are not digestible by most security logging systems (SIEM), meaning Security Operations Center teams monitoring the environment are missing critical data.

"ERP systems are incredibly complex," Aaron explained. "Normally you would do an RFP for a new service like this, but 85 percent of the Fortune 500 all use the same ERP system, and there is already a commercial solution out there that specifically addresses these challenges. But this won't be the case for most of our more complex protect surfaces. Isabelle, can you spin up a new project, please?"

"Of course," Isabelle said. "I'll pull in the ERP team and work with Purchasing."

"We'll also need to make some process changes," Aaron continued. "Dylan, I want you to work with your new friend on the finance team to negotiate a weekly maintenance window where the ERP team can begin applying patches."

"I'll talk to Donna," Dylan said.

"I'm wondering why we didn't start with identity as our primary protect surface?" Brent asked. "There is clearly a lot of work that needs to be done with Ides, but even after we do all that work, a compromised account could still cause a lot of problems, right?"

"I agree that identity is a critical service. In fact, it will be the next protect surface we address," Aaron answered. "But we started with the Ides as the first of the primary protect surfaces for one main reason. And it's the first of the Zero Trust design principles. By starting with Ides, we're focusing on the business. We're forcing ourselves to understand how the business makes money."

"I guess that makes sense," Brent conceded.

"But there's another reason I wanted to hold off on identity," Aaron said. "We're thinking of all the specific misuse cases around the ERP system. And that brings us to the next step in the Zero Trust methodology: creating policies. We need to begin building policies based on identities. So in a way, we're practicing identity now so it will be that much easier later on."

"We got MFA set up for Ides last year," Brent offered.

"What about continuous reauthentication?" asked Rose.

"Uh-oh," Aaron exclaimed. "Somebody has been reading the NIST standards."

"What's wrong with that?" Rose asked. The others all looked up at Aaron.

"It's not bad or anything," Aaron laughed. "They did a good job capturing a good conceptual framework for the architectural concepts we use in Zero Trust."

"But?" Dylan asked.

"But," Aaron said, "NIST 800-207 is focused on architecture, which is important. But there's not much guidance for what to do or where to start if you're going to do the work of maturing your information security program to embrace the strategy of Zero Trust. That's what the four design principles and the five design methodology steps give you. The design principles and methodology were developed by John Kindervag over a decade of actually doing the work of implementing successful Zero Trust projects at hundreds of companies."

"That makes sense," Dylan said.

"Sorry, dumb question, but what's a NIST?" Isabelle asked.

"It's the National Institute of Standards and Technology," Rose explained. "It's a government group that comes up with standards for almost every industry. They have a lot of standards around IT and security."

"The reason that I get frustrated with the NIST Zero Trust architecture," Aaron explained, "is that there's nothing in it about aligning with the business. Remember, Zero Trust is the strategy for preventing a security breach at your unique organization, and there are lots of ways to accomplish that. The NIST Zero Trust Architecture lists several ways to accomplish Zero Trust, but you could use any or all of those approaches in any organization. Many of the recommendations, if actually implemented, would make it harder for employees to do their work or for consumers to use your products with what is commercially available on the market. But as we start to define our Zero Trust policies for Ides, you should understand the NIST 800-207 Zero Trust Basic Tenets." Aaron waved his hand and displayed the tenets on the video wall:

- All data sources and computing services are considered resources.
- All communication is secured regardless of network location.
- Access to individual enterprise resources is granted on a per-session basis.
- Access to resources is determined by dynamic policy—including the observable state of client identity, application/service, and the requesting asset—and may include other behavioral and environmental attributes.
- The enterprise monitors and measures the integrity and security posture of all owned and associated assets.
- All resource authentication and authorization is dynamic and strictly enforced before access is allowed.
- The enterprise collects as much information as possible about the current state of assets, network infrastructure, and communications, and uses it to improve its security posture.

"Each of these tenets applies to identity and access management, or IAM," Aaron explained. "How employee logging in will need to be vetted. Again, this applies to employee IAM but not consumer IAM."

"Isn't there something called UEBA that the security guys have been talking about for a while? Is that what this is?" Dylan asked. To Isabelle he explained, "That stands for user and entity behavior analytics."

"In a way, you're right, Dylan," Aaron answered. "Many of the Zero Trust frameworks, from Gartner to Google, have come up with this idea of a policy engine. The idea is that you should be able to take the kinds of things that UEBA was supposed to give you, but instead of just reporting them to your security team, you'd be able to automatically act on that data inside your ERP system. Or any other protect surface, for that matter. In practice that's pretty hard to do. There are some companies out there building policy engines, but they don't work with every bit of software out there. At this point, we're going to do what we can inside the ERP system. But we'll be able to do more once we get to our endpoints. Remember, we're starting from the inside and working our way out to the edge."

"I've heard some people talk about assumption of breach when it comes to Zero Trust," Rose said. "But we haven't talked about that yet."

"There are some implicit assumptions that NIST creators want you to make when thinking about Zero Trust," Aaron said as he waved his hand and displayed the NIST Zero Trust view of the network:

- The entire enterprise private network is not considered an implicit trust zone.
- Devices on the network may not be owned or configurable by the enterprise.
- No resource is inherently trusted.
- Not all enterprise resources are on enterprise-owned infrastructure.
- Remote enterprise subjects and assets cannot fully trust their local network connection.
- Assets and workflows moving between enterprise and nonenterprise infrastructure should have a consistent security policy and posture.

"These are all very specific reminders that when it comes to computers or networks, you should have Zero Trusts to give. Some definitions of Zero Trust also include the idea that you should always assume that you've been breached and apply as many trusts as you would give in that situation, which is also zero. Your tech stack is always going to be evolving, so your security strategy should plan for an evolution over time of your technology and provide the equivalent level of security, regardless of whether it's on premises or in the cloud, whether it's a containerized app or a hardware appliance."

"Somebody has Zero Trust issues," Harmony joked.

"We all know by now that the final step in the Zero Trust methodology is to monitor and maintain," Aaron began. "But as we've seen with all the other parts of the ERP system, they don't work with our existing controls, and this is just as true with the ERP. Application logging isn't being sent to our centralized logging system." To Isabelle he explained, "We call that a security information and event management system, or SIEM." She nodded her thanks and he continued, "And because these alerts aren't going to the SIEM, the Security Operations Center or SOC would never get an alert that something has gone wrong. We'd be relying on the finance department to find suspicious payments or for customers to start complaining that their treadmills hadn't arrived."

"Why wouldn't the SIEM be able to receive the ERP logs?" Dylan asked.

"It wouldn't matter, because even if those logs were being sent to the SIEM, they wouldn't be able to read those logs. Most commercial SIEMs like the one we use can't understand logs from an ERP system. It would be a huge undertaking to get these into your SIEM, and when the next change happened, you'd need to start this all over again."

"So it sounds like we need yet another tool to be able to monitor all of that activity in a central place?" Isabelle asked.

"Actually, the one I had in mind bundles many of the controls that we've been talking about into a single system. And from that system you can send alerts to your SIEM so that your SOC can respond to threats in real time, as well as monitor for suspicious activity as changes are made."

Dylan looked down at his phone, which was vibrating on the table. He picked it up and unlocked it. "I just got a text from Noor," he said. "The hacker is claiming that he's stolen all of our user credentials and is offering them for sale on the dark web. Here's the tweet." Dylan sent the image to the video wall.

Tweet from 3nc0r3 publicly posting all of MarchFit's stolen data in an attempt to embarrass the company after they refused to pay the ransom

"That's all our customers," Rose said.

"Noor says the security consultant is reviewing. They're checking the dump to see if it actually contains real data or if it's bogus," Dylan said.

Key Takeaways

This chapter focused on what many organizations consider their crown jewels: their ERP and CRM systems. Some organizations use a single software provider for both of these, whereas others have the two functions separate. The unique challenges around ERP systems require highly specialized knowledge, and many smaller organizations may choose to bring in specialists to help understand the often complex environments that ERP systems can create.

According to some reports, up to 85 percent of the Fortune 500 use the popular ERP system SAP to enable their businesses to have the insights they need. And although SAP and other ERP systems can be secure, they are not necessarily secure by default. There are a number of unique challenges that these systems can create:

- Specialized programming languages are not supported by most security code review tools.
- ERP change control is often a manual process and isn't built into the ERP system itself.
- Traditional vulnerability management tools don't scan applications or code updates.
- Compliance management mechanisms, like enforcing password standards, configurations, or access to sensitive data, aren't native to ERP systems.
- Application logs are not digestible by most security logging systems (SIEM), meaning Security Operations Center teams monitoring the environment are missing critical data.

In the ERP system, it's also very important to understand how users are assigned permissions to interact with applications. The next chapter will focus on identity and Zero Trust, so it is also important to understand how some Zero Trust frameworks have integrated these two important concepts.

There have been a lot of attempts at creating a Zero Trust framework. Gartner, Forrester, and even Google have put their own spin on Zero Trust. But the NIST Zero Trust Architecture is the one that you're most likely to see in practice. In the future, vendor contracts may require companies to certify that they are

NIST 800-207 compliant, so viewing your Zero Trust implementation from a NIST perspective is an important guide for measuring success.

There are many definitions of Zero Trust. NIST defines it as follows (`https://doi.org/10.6028/NIST.SP.800-207`):

> Zero Trust (ZT) provides a collection of concepts and ideas designed to minimize uncertainty in enforcing accurate, least privilege per-request access decisions in information systems and services in the face of a network viewed as compromised. Zero Trust Architecture (ZTA) is an enterprise's cybersecurity plan that utilizes zero trust concepts and encompasses component relationships, workflow planning, and access policies. Therefore, a Zero Trust Enterprise (ZTE) is the network infrastructure (physical and virtual) and operational policies that are in place for an enterprise as a product of a zero trust architecture plan.

This definition can be rewritten as the following equation:

$$ZT + ZTA = ZTE$$

This definition was intended to add identity services (ZTA) to a network-centric view of Zero Trust. And the definition concludes that the only way to have a truly Zero Trust Enterprise (ZTE) is to have both identity as well as network controls. Because identity is so important to Zero Trust, we will discuss it in more depth in the next chapter. However, this book flows from John Kindervag's original design methodology, which flows from protect surfaces.

There are seven basic tenets of Zero Trust according to NIST 800-207:

- All data sources and computing services are considered resources.
- All communication is secured regardless of network location.
- Access to individual enterprise resources is granted on a per-session basis.
- Access to resources is determined by dynamic policy—including the observable state of client identity, application/service, and the requesting asset—and may include other behavioral and environmental attributes.
- The enterprise monitors and measures the integrity and security posture of all owned and associated assets.
- All resource authentication and authorization are dynamic and strictly enforced before access is allowed.
- The enterprise collects as much information as possible about the current state of assets, network infrastructure, and communications and uses it to improve its security posture.

There are also six challenges from a network perspective that the NIST Zero Trust Architecture document specifically addresses, and that every Zero Trust project will need to address:

- The entire enterprise private network is not considered an implicit trust zone.
- Devices on the network may not be owned or configurable by the enterprise.
- No resource is inherently trusted.
- Not all enterprise resources are on enterprise-owned infrastructure.
- Remote enterprise subjects and assets cannot fully trust their local network connection.
- Assets and workflows moving between enterprise and nonenterprise infrastructure should have a consistent security policy and posture.

Chapter 5
The Identity Cornerstone

A man in a black suit and black tie was sitting at the conference room table in the briefing center with his hands steepled. The Zero Trust team was gathered around the table, and Brent was standing at the video wall in front of a picture of the MarchFit data center.

"Bob clearly is a rogue insider, but he was more than that; he was a ronin. A ninja," Brent said, gesturing to the ceiling tiles along the row of cabinets. "He must have trained all his life in both ninjutsu and the dark arts of hacking. He would have had to sneak into the data center through the air ducts, then descend down through the vents and put the USB drive hidden inside his katana into the server."

"Bob is a terrible name for a ninja," Harmony observed.

"No one would expect a ninja named Bob," Brent agreed. "Which is what makes it the perfect name for a ninja."

The man in the black suit spoke up. "That's cute. Would you like to make it interesting?"

"Sure, wise guy," Brent said.

"How about a coffee?" the suit responded.

Brent looked at the coffee machine in the lobby of the briefing center and shrugged. "Deal. What's your theory?"

The man in the black suit stood up, went to the video wall, and pulled up a picture of Bob. "Bob Paulson was one of the original employees of MarchFit. His stock had finally vested, and he left the company voluntarily over the summer to move to another startup. He would have had a lot to lose from the company experiencing a breach, but that by itself doesn't mean he didn't do it." A smug grin went over Brent's face at this, but the suit continued.

"What we do know for sure was that somehow, Bob's account was used to access the source code repository for the treadmills, which is weird, because he left the company several months ago and you would have expected that his account would have been terminated by the identity management system."

"Hey, Brent, aren't you on the identity team?" Rose asked sweetly. He had folded his arms and was staring back at her.

"It turns out that Bob wasn't just a developer at MarchFit; he was also a client. We know for sure that, although he could still be a ninja, Bob wasn't in the data center at the time because he was running on his treadmill about 1,200 miles from here."

"Why wasn't his access revoked like normal?" Dylan asked.

"Our understanding is that MarchFit's identity management system only has one domain that mixes customer and employee data in the same place. So although the process to terminate access was triggered, it failed because he was an active customer. He retained all the same permissions that he had while he was an employee. When he clicked a phishing email last month, the cybercriminal was able to get access. And since Bob was working out at the time, when he got the two-factor request to his phone, he thought it was legitimate and approved the access. Brent, I'll take a cappuccino with two sugars. Thanks."

"How do you know?" Brent asked.

"Oh, didn't you realize? He's the FBI agent in charge of our case." Dylan laughed. "This is Agent Paul Smecker. Noor asked him to debrief us on the current status of the investigation since she thought it might help us focus our efforts."

Nigel patted Brent on the back as he headed toward to the coffee machine in the other room.

"Perfect timing actually," Aaron said. "Okay, it's never a good time to have a compromised account, but identity was the next protect surface that we needed to work on. Identity is one of the most important parts of Zero Trust. Zero Trust consumes identity to help ensure least privilege. But identity is also one of your most important protect surfaces, so you need to protect it just as well as your other critical assets. I would actually argue that while your ERP is your crown, the jewels are the people. Who remembers the first Zero Trust design principle?"

"Understand the business," Rose replied.

"How does identity impact the business?" Aaron asked.

"Knowing who your customers are allows you to create a more personalized experience that better meets their needs," Rose said. "We retain our customers longer than our competitors, and our personalized experience means we give more of what we want to our audience."

"It also allows you to build security into the product," Aaron added. "The protect surface in this case isn't just one identity domain, however. It's two. There's this old saying: Hackers want access, and your employees have it. When you look at the Lockheed Martin Cyber Kill Chain, identity is the single biggest target. In the reconnaissance phase, cybercriminals will exhaustively research your employees and send mass phishing attempts to validate which ones are active and attempt to read their email to get even more insight into how your organization works. In the infiltration phase, they will attempt to spear phish IT admins or executives and attempt to move laterally to discover what assets their stolen credentials will get them. In the exploitation phase, they might attempt to brute force domain admin accounts from within your network, make fake account requests, or potentially create their own accounts if they've compromised the directory."

"It's a dirty job, but someone has to do it," Brent said.

"In the spirit of limiting the blast radius of an attack," Aaron continued, "the first thing that we'll need to do is to create separate identity domains for customers and employees. These two areas should never overlap."

"I've been saying this for years," Brent said walking back in, coffee cup in hand. "We've always been told it would be too expensive to make the change."

"We've already begun forcing all our users to change their passwords after the hacker's tweet," Isabelle said. "Sixty percent of our users have already made the change. Will this mean we have to make them change their passwords again?"

"Instead of moving your customers out of the domain you already have and creating a new one for them, we'll create a fresh domain for employees," Aaron said. "We'll do this for several reasons. Consumers are reluctant to accept any changes to their service, so there's less risk this way. At the same time, we'll want to increase security protections for our employees. And, of course, we'll be ensuring that all former employee accounts are removed."

"Brent, I think I'll need your help capturing this for a project request," Isabelle said. Brent stood behind Isabelle as she began creating a project charter.

"While they work on the project request, let's talk about the next step in the process: mapping transaction flows," Aaron said, pulling up another diagram into the video wall. "Usually this part can take up to a year to flesh out all of the ways data is being used in your environment. Fortunately for us, the hard work has already been done because of your GDPR data mapping project that was completed last year." Aaron displayed a spreadsheet with hundreds of rows of data flows through the organization and which roles in the organization have access to that data.

Isabelle leaned over to Dylan. "GDPR is that new European privacy law," she said proudly.

"How does this help us?" Harmony asked Aaron.

"The goal of identity is to ensure uniqueness of every human or nonhuman in our environment," Brent said, looking up from Isabelle's computer. "The best way to ensure we're employing least privilege across all our systems is to start with the data, what services are connected to the data, and then decide who needs access to it. Right, Aaron?"

"That's surprisingly on point, Brent," Aaron observed. "And since we'll be starting over with our employee accounts, we should also address the process for provisioning new accounts. Since we're setting up a new identity domain, we also have an opportunity to provide more secure authentication methods for employees. We can require granular authentication methods per user or role. But we also need to require users to register multiple authentication methods. When an authentication method is not available for a user, they can choose to authenticate with another method. We'll always require password, security questions, and email address, but we can also choose an app on their smartphone like Google or Microsoft Authenticator, OATH hardware tokens, SMS, voice calling, or application passwords."

"Ideally," Brent added, "we wouldn't use SMS or voice calls for employees since we know calls can be intercepted or phones can be cloned using SIM-jacking."

"What's SIM-jacking?" Rose asked.

"It's where a criminal calls your cell phone carrier pretending to be you," Brent explained. "They'll say you got a new phone, and then start getting all your text messages sent to their burner phone. Most people won't notice anything's wrong until they need to make a phone call and their cell service no longer works."

"SMS is probably fine for consumer applications. But the idea is to consider all the ways that authentication can fail before the failure happens," Aaron said. "And while we're talking about the provisioning process, we should also plan for the deprovisioning process."

"You mean when someone gets fired?" Harmony asked.

"Well, yes, although most employees leave voluntarily. But we'll also need to make sure that when someone changes jobs within the company, they don't retain access that is no longer needed," Aaron said. "How do you get your users their account information and set passwords? How do you set up your password challenge questions? How do you enroll users in MFA?"

Brent considered this for a moment. "Initially, HR will process the paperwork for a new hire. We'll send them login instructions to their personal email, and then send a one-time password to their cell phone. It's not 100 percent secure, but it is using separate channels. After that they have to change their password. They have to enroll in MFA at the same time."

"This will be one of the areas where we have an opportunity to remove trust," Aaron said. "How do we know that the new employee's personal email account hasn't been compromised? We don't. So when we build the account claiming process, we can ask the users to validate their identity by asking them to answer three or four questions that they would have provided during the hiring process."

"Isn't this a productivity issue?" Rose asked. "I mean, with the pandemic and all, I've heard some employees may be paid for weeks with nothing to do while they wait for their permissions to get assigned. Some supervisors have said they share their passwords with employees just so they can get the work done."

"That will be one of the biggest goals with Project Zero Trust," Aaron said. "We'll need to be able to make sure that any identity has the right permissions at the right time and with the right context. We'll need to implement automated feeds from the HR system to assign permissions at least daily, but maybe even hourly. This will help us react to changes to the identity life cycle in near real time and will help strengthen our security posture. And in real life, humans use other humans to delegate or proxy access to. Identity needs to help with this. The president needs to delegate access and authority to his vice president when he's on vacation, for example."

"Does this mean we've already started architecting the environment?" Harmony asked.

"You're right," Aaron said. "Now that we're talking about how we go about creating identities, we've entered into the third step of the Zero Trust methodology. We know that the third step is to architect your Zero Trust environment, but I want to make sure you are prepared to do this part on your own since it's easy to get confused when you come to a new protect surface and you're not sure how to apply the methodology. What principles do you follow when you do Zero Trust architecture?"

"We focus on eliminating trust," Dylan said.

"Exactly," Aaron responded. "When we looked at firewall rules, we got rid of rules based on IP addresses because the bad guys are great at finding those and exploiting them to get full access to a server, for example. We installed next-gen antivirus because we don't trust applications and we don't give users local admin rights because we know that attackers will install malware that way. When we look at safelist files or applications, we got rid of those because the bad guys are experts at detecting those exceptions and using them like a Trojan horse to install malware."

"Trust is a vulnerability," Brent said.

"Right again," Aaron continued. "When we look at our most critical systems, we know that we have blind spots. Sometimes we need tools to help us detect those blind spots and often we need to lean on our business partners to help us have an attitudinal perspective that can overcome blind spots in the future."

"So what does this have to do with identity?" Harmony asked.

"Identity is one of those highly technical areas where it's easy to get lost in the details and lose sight of the big picture. With identity, we have built-in blind spots. It's easy to think of my digital identity as an extension of myself. But it's not like the movie *Tron* where there are little people inside a computer hanging out with each other and having conversations. Were the people in *The Matrix* really in the matrix? Of course not, there are no humans in computer networks. While we may use identities to uniquely identify our users, those identities aren't our users. Therefore, as we architect our Zero Trust protect surface for identities, we shouldn't trust identities."

"So it's like the woman in the red dress," Brent said.

"I don't get it," Rose admitted.

"That was Neo's final lesson in *The Matrix*," Brent explained. "He wasn't really in *The Matrix* at that point. In a way, that was like a man-in-the-middle attack."

"Wait, how do we do identity if we don't trust identity?" Harmony asked.

"We have to start at the beginning of the identity life cycle and look for opportunities to remove trust from the equation. For customers, this might mean adding an 'I'm not a robot' button to ensure that it isn't a bot enrolling in the service. For employees or contractors, there may be a different process to start the provisioning process. And whenever we think about provisioning," Aaron said, "we have to consider deprovisioning at the same time. Even if a team member is just changing jobs inside MarchFit, we still need to make sure their permissions don't just keep ballooning bigger and bigger over time. And like we saw with Bob, there are a lot of security risks with orphaned accounts. Isabelle, as we create the charter for the new employee identity domain, we'll need to ensure that we're including automated provisioning and deprovisioning of accounts with the help of adjacent and applicable business processes. Automating this process will allow us to get the full value out of our identity system by reducing the number of manual access changes, reducing the potential for error or outright fraud."

"How granular do we need to be with provisioning access for Zero Trust?" Brent asked. "Normally we grant permission based on user roles, but we could always have more customized permissions."

"Remember, the goal of Zero Trust is to prevent breaches. But with identity, there is a balancing act that we have to do. It's true that more customization can provide more security, but it also makes it harder to automate and thus introduces more room for error. I think you're right to bring this up now, since as the company has grown, more and more roles became separate, so a role cleanup is probably in order at this point. Isabelle, please add that to the project charter as well."

"I'm getting the impression that the identity project is going to be the longest part of Project Zero Trust," Dylan said.

"In some organizations, a Zero Trust initiative can take two to three years," Aaron admitted. "But you've got a lot of the key elements already in place. The GDPR assessment, for example, probably took about a year off that time frame. Identity will consume a lot of hours, but it can also be done in parallel with the other areas that we'll work on. So we'll still be able to make our six-month goal for the project."

"What other things do we need to consider when it comes to identity?" Rose asked.

"What about Single Sign On?" Dylan asked.

"We've already rolled out SSO to several of our major applications," Brent said. "But the various parts of the organization have over two hundred different unique services that we support, some with unique logins that aren't even a part of our identity system. MFA is already integrated with SSO. As a part of the conversion to the new IAM domain for employees, if we required SSO for all our applications we could speed up the adoption of both SSO and MFA."

"You can also use something like a WAF on your SSO page to help detect credential stuffing attacks where cybercriminals have stolen usernames and passwords on other sites and try to use them on yours," Agent Smecker said. "Unfortunately, this works very often since users don't use unique passwords on all the sites they use."

"Brent, are you using any federation in your identity system?" Aaron asked.

"Not today," Brent said. "But I see where you're going with that. If we move our employees to a new domain, that would allow us to give our customers the option to bring their own identity from their email provider or social media site. We couldn't let that happen with our employees, so we've always been anti-federation."

"Like the Klingons," Harmony joked. After no one laughed she said, "What, a room full of nerds and no Trekkies? Ugh." She pulled her hoodie over her head and resumed typing.

Isabelle lowered the screen on her laptop. "Is that all there is for the identity project?"

"There are still a couple things we'll need to talk about," Aaron answered. "Brent, what are you doing for PAM?"

"Who's Pam?" Rose asked.

"We don't have a PAM system yet," Brent admitted.

"OK, what's PAM?" Rose asked.

Brent leaned back in his seat. "Privileged access management is used to manage the superuser accounts that IT administrators use to control servers and other systems. These should be kept separate from their normal, everyday accounts that they use for email. Admin-level accounts are one of the primary targets for cybercriminals, so having a system to manage them more closely is critical. A PAM system can rotate passwords for admin accounts much more frequently than a normal account, and audit controls can be configured much more tightly. I always thought PAM was cool, but we've always been too busy with product releases and testing to get much traction there."

"What do we do today?" Dylan asked.

"Oh, we do have separate email accounts and admin accounts for all IT staff. They use their admin account to perform any administrative tasks, and that account doesn't have an email associated with it. But there are also PAM tools for admins to have a temp login, and that can be another project that gets spun up."

"That's good," Aaron said. "They can do a lot with just a normal employee account. But like we saw with Bob the cyber ninja, they can do almost anything with an admin account."

"I thought MFA was supposed to fix all that," Harmony said.

Brent sat up again. "MFA ensures that the user making the authentication request is who they say they are, because the user must input an additional token that is generated on another device they own. The secondary factors used in MFA policies are much more difficult to spoof because they are time-sensitive and generally tied to hardware that an attacker is less likely to get their hands on. But it's not impossible. I guess sometimes users do click the second-factor request even when they shouldn't."

"How does failure work with MFA?" Aaron asked. "What happens if a user has a lost or stolen phone? Or what if they get a new device?"

"We ask them to save a backup code or call the help desk," Brent said.

"Wait, how are they supposed to call the help desk if they don't have a phone?" Harmony asked. "Or what if they saved their backup code on their phone?"

"Well, they can always just reset their password and re-enroll their new phone once they get it," Brent said.

"But they can't work in the meantime," Rose said.

"This is another great opportunity to remove trust from the identity process. One of the most common ways attackers compromise accounts is through resetting a user's password. Usually, the challenge questions we ask are easily guessable. I actually recommend that we require an MFA reauthentication before a user can change a password to ensure they are the one making the request."

"Why don't we just require MFA everywhere and force everyone to reauthenticate hourly," Nigel said. "Wouldn't that fix everything?"

"Unfortunately, no," Aaron answered. "Agent Smecker, can you talk about the ways that cybercriminals get around MFA?"

"Sure," Agent Smecker began. "Let's say this cyber ninja, Bob, needs to break into an organization. Since Bob is a ninja, we can assume he's already compromised the username and password. Bob has three ways to deal with MFA. He can disable or weaken MFA. He can directly bypass MFA. Or he can exploit an existing exception to MFA."

"Wait, I thought multifactor authentication was supposed to be secure?" Harmony asked.

"It certainly raises the degree of difficulty," Agent Smecker answered, and took another sip of his cappuccino. "But like Brent said, this guy is probably a ninja. To disable or weaken MFA, he might choose to modify some trusted IP address configurations inside MarchFit, for example. Or if he wanted to bypass MFA altogether, he can use SMS intercepts like you've already mentioned. Or he could compromise the device a user has already authenticated with MFA."

"You said there was a third way that he can get around MFA?" Dylan asked.

"That's right. He can exploit authorized MFA exceptions. Bob would identify an account operating without MFA requirements like a service account, and attack them directly. Or much more commonly, Bob could target legacy applications like POP or IMAP, which don't support MFA. You'd be shocked at how much info a cybercriminal can glean from reading your email."

"What about stolen certs and session reuse?" Dylan asked.

"As a technique," Agent Smecker began, "stolen certificates have been known for a while. But it's been talked about a lot lately because it was used in the Solar-Winds breach. Basically, all an attacker needs to do is steal the private key to sign certificates. Another variation is the golden ticket attack, where the attacker uses a forged key that lets them control any resource in an Active Directory domain. It's like the golden ticket in Willy Wonka, except once you get in, there aren't any Oompa Loompas escorting you around; you can go wherever you want."

"We'll work on this part when we get to the monitor and maintain step," Aaron interrupted, "but this technique is a real challenge to detect since the requests look legitimate. But you were going to talk about session reuse as well?"

"This is like the MFA bypass scenario I talked about before. A cybercriminal will compromise a device with an existing authenticated session. Most MFA configurations have a default thirty-day period before they require the user to reauthenticate because they don't want to negatively impact user productivity. This gives the threat actor a window in which they can establish more permanent access into the network."

"How often should users be required to reauthenticate?" Dylan asked.

"We don't have a lot of official data around this, but for higher-security areas some organizations require reauthentication every time a user logs in, which could be lots of times per day. Daily works for a lot of organizations because it's a more predictable user experience. But for consumers, it might be much less."

"Oh, sorry, guys, I've got to run to our Identity Governance meeting," Brent said.

"Perfect timing, actually," Aaron said. "Dylan, you and Isabelle should tag along with Brent to get their input on some of the changes we're talking about. But the real goal will be to get their help in defining our Zero Trust identity policies."

Brent was out of breath when they reached the conference room. The wall facing the hallway was all glass while the outer wall had windows facing the courtyard. The large conference table seated twelve people, but only a few seats had been taken. Brent said, "Tell them I'll be a second, I just need to grab something," and disappeared down the hallway into a maze of cubicles.

Isabelle held the door for Dylan and he walked in. It was unusually hot in the room. Noor was talking quietly to Kofi at the other side of the room. Kim Self had just started the Zoom session and several people appeared on the large TV at the end of the table. She was fanning herself with a piece of paper. Instead of closing the door, Isabelle propped it open, then walked to the other side of the glass wall that ran along the hallway and propped the other door open.

A tall man that Brent hadn't seen before went over to a tall bladeless fan in the corner of the room and switched it on. He held his hand out to make sure air was moving, then put his face to the fan. "Please don't tell me someone hacked the air conditioning, too," he said.

"Don't say that. The hackers might be listening," Dylan joked, but stopped short when the man didn't smile. "I'm Dylan," he said, extending his hand.

"Hi, Dylan. Olivia has told me a lot about you," the man said, taking Dylan's hand firmly. "I'm Victor Vega. But please, everyone calls me Vic."

"Oh, you know Olivia?" Dylan said, surprised.

"She's kinda my boss. I run our sales team," Vic said.

Isabelle appeared beside Vic with a thin woman behind her. "Oh good, you've met Vic. Let me also introduce you to Mia; she's our head of human resources."

"Mia Wallace. Nice to meet you, Dylan," she said, shaking his hand. "I didn't realize that you'd be joining us today."

Dylan was about to speak when Brent came in, carrying a large chocolate Bundt cake. There were several yelps of joy from around the room at seeing the cake. Dylan turned to Isabelle, confused at this new side of Brent. Isabelle shrugged.

"Brent's the man!" Vic said.

"I know, I know," Brent said, turning to Dylan. "I promised I'd bake a cake when we finally finished our user access review workflow," he said in explanation as Noor took the cake from him. "We'll be ready to start next week."

"I really miss starting meetings out on a positive note," Noor said as she cut a slice. "Sorry for the folks working remote today. We'll save a slice for you. For the folks who've not had the pleasure of meeting him yet, Dylan is here today to give us an update on Project Zero Trust."

"Thank you, Dr. Patel," Dylan said, regretting that he had just taken a bite of cake. It was delicious and he chewed for a few seconds before continuing. "We've started focusing on our highest-priority applications, and identity is one of the most important parts of any Zero Trust strategy. We're working with Isabelle to formally launch some identity-related projects, but we'll need this group's help in order to craft our policies."

"The goal of this Identity Governance group," Noor said, "has always been to secure our data while ensuring a seamless user experience and compliance. We know that having a team of IAM stakeholders is critical to the success of our identity program. We need to hear what's foremost on your minds."

"What about reducing our costs?" Vic asked. "This Zero Trust project isn't cheap on top of what we're paying to clean up the hacks. I'm worried all these costs will impact our new product launch."

"I'm less concerned about costs than I am about the damage to our brand," April said. "If the new product launch is to be successful, we have to demonstrate that we've made real changes."

"One big part of the identity project will be a role cleanup," Brent answered. "We want to make sure that every user in our organization has a role assigned to them that's independent of their title. Those roles will have permission to access resources based on the job description. We know that in our early startup days, permissions were given to lots of people, and standardizing those permissions will help us automate the process of bringing new people on board."

"That sounds like you'll need a lot of help from HR," Mia said.

"We'll work with your business leads, Mia," Brent said. "But the idea will be that we need to tie all accounts to an owner, manager, or sponsor of some kind. As we go through all of those accounts, we'll be looking for orphaned accounts or accounts where the password has expired, and we'll need someone to talk to before we remove them. But also, they need to know what specific permissions the account really needs. I can think of lots of cases where the person requesting an account asked for too many permissions out of fear or lack of knowledge. This should fix that."

Kofi cleared his throat and waited for the room's attention. "The consultant's report indicated that the cybercriminal had been inside our network for months even though we had multifactor authentication in place. I found the passage stating that some systems allowed you to stay logged in indefinitely particularly concerning."

"That was one of the policy items we wanted your help with. We need to make sure all applications are required to use MFA and make it a part of all applications by default before they're rolled out. But we also want to require users to reauthenticate daily, or even more frequently when doing a particularly important transaction, like authorizing a payment or deploying code into production, for example."

"I actually really like that idea," April said. "Sometimes when we have blackout windows that are set by the SEC, we need to make sure we don't accidentally disclose information for insider trading purposes. I'd love to have a reauthentication point before one of my team members can publish certain documents to the site. That wouldn't get in the way at all."

"Brent made this?" Harmony asked as she took a bite of the Bundt cake. "OMG, this is good. Didn't see that coming."

"Brent mentioned they were in the process of launching a user access review process next week," Dylan said.

"That's perfect," Aaron said. "And that actually brings us to the final step for the protect surface for identity: monitoring. User access reviews are a big part of that. Usually, users' access privileges are reviewed on a regular basis, like monthly or quarterly to make sure only the right people have continued access."

"Brent said they'd start at quarterly and planned to increase the frequency as the identity team worked through issues," Isabelle said, then continued eating her own slice of cake. "I can't believe how good this cake is. Would it be weird if I asked for the recipe?"

"Access reviews should also be triggered when any employee is promoted or transferred where access change occurs," Aaron said. "Making your IAM program an integral part of all new application onboarding/major change discussions will also mean that all identity activity can be monitored in one central repository and correlated with other security events more easily."

"Remind me again how monitoring is related to Zero Trust?" Brent asked, coming back into the room. "Isn't this something the Security Operations Center is supposed to do?"

"There are two main aspects of how your Zero Trust strategy plays out in practice," Aaron explained. "First, it forces visibility into your environment and prevents bad things from happening. But we also don't trust that we got everything right the first time or that nothing changed without us knowing. So our Zero Trust methodology also needs to be able to detect when things go wrong. Obviously all identity components need to feed into your SIEM or UEBA tools. But we should also enable both basic and advanced auditing as well as monitoring for object and attribute changes in the directory."

"Didn't we talk about UEBA the other day when you talked about the policy engine thing from the NIST standard?" Dylan asked.

"UEBA is really interesting," Aaron said, "but what we really need when it comes to identity are integrations that share signals for identity. This is actually why the Identity Defined Security Alliance, or IDSA, has developed a framework to apply Zero Trust to each stage of the identity life cycle. The seven identity components are Identity, Device, Network, Compute, Application, Storage, and Data. The idea is that these seven components make up all of the different interactions a user could have in an environment, and each of these different areas should be able to send or receive signals to the policy engine. But these are the seven areas we'll need to ensure that we have visibility into to be able to successfully monitor and maintain the strategy as well."

Aaron displayed the IDSA reference architecture document. "Sometimes you have a user passing through all these layers to get to the data. Other times, a process inside an application will use a service account through the network to access the data."

"It seems like for every new protect surface from here on out, we'll want to build identity into the Zero Trust process so that we'll be looking at the complete end-to-end authentication process?" Dylan asked.

	Client "Device"			Network	Server/Service "Device"		
"Users" = Humans Bots Processes Code	Application	Compute	Storage		Application	Compute	Storage
	IDENTITY						Data
	Access Management (AM)						
	Multi-Factor Authentication (MFA)						
	Privileged Access Management (PAM)						
	Directory Services (DS)						
	Identity Governance & Administration (IGA)						
	CONTEXT, RISK, POLICY, WORKFLOW						
	Unified Endpoint Management (UEM)				Cloud Access Security Broker (CASB)		
	Data Leakage Prevention (DLP)				Online Fraud Detection (OFD)		
	Software Defined Perimeter (SDP)				Data Access Governance (DAG)		
	Other...				Other...		
	Security Information & Event Management (SIEM...+UEBA...+SOAR)						
	SECURITY						

Identity-defined security reference architecture
Courtesy Identity Defined Security Alliance

"Exactly," Aaron said. "Ensure you're consuming all the elements of identity. You should be using identity in your firewall rules, at a minimum. But as you work with the Identity Governance group, you should also identify opportunities for reauthentication for each protect surface that will be frictionless to the end user."

"There's another tweet from the hacker, Encore. It's like his name is designed to get more annoying the more he hacks you," Harmony said as she scrolled through her messages.

"How do you know?" Brent asked.

"I started following him on Twitter," Harmony said. "What?" she said at his surprised look. "Was I not supposed to?"

> **3nc0r3**
> @3nc0r32
>
> Had spare time, found 3 0-days going thru @MarchFit code. Let the bidding begin!
>
> 3:53 PM · Oct 11, 2022 · Twitter Web App
>
> **6.8K** Retweets   **792** Quote Tweets   **19.5K** Likes

Tweet from the hacker 3nc0r3 claiming that he had found three zero days in MarchFit's code offering to sell to the highest bidder.

"I started following him too," Rose said.

"That's fine, it's smart. I wish I had thought of it already," Dylan admitted.

"Oh no," Harmony sighed. "If you dig into the threads, he says one of the zero days would allow cybercriminals access to the camera to view inside people's homes."

Key Takeaways

While your ERP system may be your crown, the jewels are the people connected with your organization. With identity there aren't people inside the network like in *The Matrix*. It's tempting to "trust" an identity, but with Zero Trust, the goal is to prevent and contain breaches by removing trust wherever possible. In practice, this can be done in a number of ways, but since identity is what enables your people to do their jobs or enables your customers to engage with you, it must be done in as seamless a manner as possible.

Identity requires a much more comprehensive understanding of how the business works than traditional technology services. Identity drives the business, offering not just authentication services to protect data but also helping the business connect with customers and provide more personalized services. Process always comes before technology. It's always more important to understand why a process needs to be in place before the technology is deployed for that task. The good news, however, is that most likely some of this work has already been done. Many organizations have done GDPR, HIPAA, or CCPA assessments, and these assessments can help jump-start the data flow mapping process that the Zero Trust methodology requires.

One of the most important criteria for a successful identity program is to have an Identity Governance group that meets regularly. This group should be made up of business owners and include representatives from HR, Legal, Risk, Privacy, and IT. This group should define owners of identity and ensure that the identity program objectives are aligned to business priorities.

The cornerstone of any cloud security strategy is identity. While we will focus on cloud in a later chapter, your legacy on-premises technology environment has relied for years on firewalls or other controls at Internet egress points. Those controls are no longer effective when it comes to the cloud. Many workers are now able to work remotely, so it's more important than ever to eliminate the "chewy centers" of our legacy networks that John Kindervag described in his original paper where he proposed a Zero Trust approach to security.

Getting identity right in cloud environments is critical for both service delivery and protecting the data that runs the business. In the cloud, identity provides the foundation of the majority of your security assurances.

As Agent Smecker illustrates in the story, getting identity right also means being able to provide answers after something bad happens. The Identity Defined Security Alliance (IDSA) has a framework of the seven components of a digital system that consume identity. How each of these elements interacts with identity in your environment determines the identity-defined security approaches that you can use to construct your Zero Trust strategy. The seven IDSA components are:

- Identity
- Device
- Network
- Compute
- Application
- Storage
- Data

For all protect surfaces, the complete end-to-end authentication process for how identity is consumed should be detailed in the data flow mapping stage of the Zero Trust methodology. The goal will be twofold: First, you should ensure that you're consuming all the elements of identity and leveraging them when creating Zero Trust policies in each protect surface; second, for each flow, and with the help of the business owner of that identity, you should identify opportunities for reauthentication that will be frictionless to the end user.

Chapter 6
Zero Trust DevOps

Dylan had to duck into a corner to get out of the way of the movers rolling the red tool chests out of Olivia's old office. He was able to inch a little further before the next group of movers hauled the red couch away as well. Once they were out of the way, he went into the large corner office to find Vic pacing along the windows of the office. The room was now full of plastic-wrapped furniture. Dylan was about to speak when Vic held up his hand and began talking. It took a moment before Dylan realized Vic had his wireless headphones in and was speaking with someone else.

The last several days had been a whirlwind. Olivia called an all-hands meeting just a couple days after the cybercriminal's last tweet, and she had announced that she was stepping down from her role as CEO. She thanked everyone for their support and announced that Victor Vega was going to be the interim CEO while the company conducted a national search. The most important thing, she emphasized, was that she didn't want any distractions from their new product launch. Even her.

"Tell them we're going to need double the number of orders to meet expectations. This will be our chance to do something revolutionary and we're not going to shoot ourselves in the foot by not having enough on day one to meet demand," Vic said to the person on the phone.

Vic was the natural person to step up and assume the role. He had been at the company since the beginning and everyone assumed he'd take over the role as CEO when Olivia retired. And now the new CEO was calling Dylan in for a meeting.

"Make them believe, Cecilia. We're not selling Iron Man suits, but this is the next best thing," Vic said, and tapped his phone to hang up and walked over to shake Dylan's hand. "Alone at last," he said, tossing his blazer onto the top of the desk.

"Yes, we were giving Olivia regular reports on the status of Project Zero Trust. I can get you up to speed now if you want," Dylan offered.

"That's not why I called you in. Sorry, there's no place to sit down yet," Vic said, going to the window. Dylan followed. The view was spectacular with the leaves starting to change colors and fall.

"Security is costing us too much money, Dylan. This hacker thing is costing us millions to clean up right when we need to focus. Our investors are getting nervous. We planned to go IPO after the new product launched, and to make that happen we need people to believe we can turn this ship around. I'll be honest with you, everything is riding on the new product. If it doesn't blow people's minds, there's a good shot we go out of business. And we need to free up funds to make that happen."

"Wait, does that mean you're killing Project Zero Trust?" Dylan asked.

"What? No. I expect results from your little project. I've read your reports, and I believe you're ready to finish the job. You've had a blank check so far and that has to change. I'm starting with the expensive consultant you've had training you for the past two months. Your team needs to vacate the briefing center, we need to start hosting meetings there again. And it's time you started working to secure our new product as well, that should be your focus right now."

"We've got to show not just that the product is amazing," Dylan said, "but that our next generation of customers can trust us enough to continue or even increase their subscriptions with us. Security is a part of the product. That's what we've failed to understand. I am to correct that. But we have to make the product secure with what we have."

"You've got it exactly right, Dylan," Vic said.

A few minutes later, Dylan and Aaron were walking together down a row of cubicles.

"Okay, but I don't know what the new product is," Dylan said. Aaron had met him after the meeting with Vic and they were walking back to the briefing center. "People keep talking about it like it's a secret. And I didn't want to ask about it if I wasn't supposed to know. I figured someone would tell me eventually. But then, after a while, it seemed too embarrassing to ask."

Aaron started laughing hysterically, crumpling over against the wall to catch his breath.

"Of course it's a secret, but this isn't Apple. Zero Trust isn't about not trusting people, it's about not trusting computers. But still, it's a good sign for you that MarchFit does have some good operational security."

"Okay, so what is it?" Dylan asked as they walked back into the lobby on the way to the front of the building.

"Oh, no. You're not getting off that easy. You'll have to talk to your CTO."

"We have a CTO? How am I just now finding that out?" Dylan exclaimed.

"He's one of those DevOps guys. They're like the Ricky Bobbies of the technology world," Aaron said.

"What's that supposed to mean?"

"Ricky Bobby just wants to go fast." Aaron chuckled as he said it. "Most security teams work for the CIO and are internally focused. CTOs are usually focused on the customers outside the organization. But the MarchFit app and the hardware need Zero Trust as well. DevOps is actually a great fit for Zero Trust because the process is already so well defined. This protect surface should be easy for you. You should grab Nigel and head over to meet Boris," Aaron said as they reached the front doors. Dylan realized that this might be the last time they spoke.

"You knew? I thought you'd be more upset about leaving," Dylan said.

"Two months is a lot of time to get up to speed on Zero Trust. You've got the right team around you. I figured this might be time for me to go spread the gospel of Zero Trust to other clients. But I'll tell you what. You can call me three times after I leave, no charge."

A few minutes later, Dylan and Nigel were sitting in the waiting room outside Boris' office. "You've got to be kidding me," Dylan said.

"Our customers are all folks who are working from home. People aren't leaving their houses as much as they used to and VR is taking off. So having a 360-degree treadmill at their desk will still allow them to walk during business hours, but then they could watch TV or movies or play games while they run. Kids could go to virtual schools like in *Ready Player One*. You could run alongside your favorite basketball player during the game."

"I thought you guys would be more upset about getting kicked out of the briefing center," Dylan said apologetically.

"It was nice while it lasted. But we knew it wasn't going to last," Nigel said as the door to the CTO's office opened.

Dylan followed Nigel into the darkened room. The only light in the room came from the cluster of computer monitors behind Boris and the blue lights from a fish tank that took up the entire wall on the other side of the room. There was a stick of incense burning behind Boris, giving the room a cinnamon and lavender smell. Dylan couldn't be sure, but it looked like the smoke detectors had been wrapped in aluminum foil.

"Did you know that 90 percent of the value of the S&P 500 is made up of intellectual property?" Boris asked. "That's what we're creating here. I trust all my developers to create value for the company. Nobody writes perfect code, but I think we should be measured on whether we can rise to meet a challenge. And because we have a DevOps shop, we were able to patch your hacker's zero-day vulnerabilities within forty-eight hours. At another company, we might have been struggling to patch six months from now."

"That's incredible. Your team is amazing," Dylan admitted.

"So what I'm most concerned about is the intellectual property theft here. What if our code was leaked to a competitor? What if our code was used by a criminal to hack our customers?"

"We're hoping to do something about that," Dylan said.

"I've heard about that. But you know what I think? Zero Trust is just a fad, we can't operate without trust," Boris said. "We rely on our people to solve problems every day. My developers won't work someplace where Big Brother is always watching them."

"Zero Trust doesn't mean we shouldn't trust people," Dylan said. "We're actually here to get to know more about you and your team. Tell me more about what makes your team successful."

"We've adopted a DevOps model to deliver software to our treadmill network," Boris said. "We're pushing hundreds of code updates every week."

"That's incredible," Dylan admitted.

"We can't do anything that will slow that down," Boris said.

"Understood," Dylan said. "We're here to help find ways to secure our code, but one of the first steps is to understand the process and how information flows through the organization."

"Maybe start with the code repository?" Nigel suggested.

"Let me start at a high level and then work my way to that," Boris said. "DevOps is about eliminating barriers between developers and operations. You should definitely read *The Phoenix Project* if you haven't already. It's like a religion for some. But the secret is that it relies on having the right tools in place to help teams rapidly and reliably deploy and innovate. There's a tech stack, and as Nigel indicated, it starts with the code repository."

"That's where we keep the code?" Dylan asked.

"It does more than just store the code," Boris said. "It handles version control and allows developers to collaborate on projects."

"Where does it go from there?"

"The next step is the continuous integration and continuous delivery pipeline. When patches are sent, the code repository calls the CI/CD tool and this tool is what builds the application into a container. The container gets pushed out via our orchestration tool. And the whole thing is hosted in the cloud."

"That's really helpful. How do your developers log in to all those applications?" Dylan asked. "We've been able to use our stronger identity protections to help secure processes from end to end. Are all of these DevOps tools using our identity system?"

"It takes too long to get accounts from operations," Boris said. "We set up all the accounts ourselves."

"Does that mean there are separate logins for each tool the developers have to use?" Dylan asked. Boris crossed his arms and nodded.

"Hey, boss," Nigel began. "Wouldn't it be a great process improvement if our developers didn't have to log in to their accounts like fifty times a day? Dylan, for one code change, I might have to log in to all of these systems separately and they all use different passwords. I use a password manager, but some guys still type them from memory. I bet I spend twenty minutes a day just typing passwords."

"Yes. Yes," Boris answered. "This would help us go faster. I never trusted the identity system since we mixed customer and employee data. Thought it would be better to use local accounts. But now that we're separated, I'm open to this."

"Great," Dylan said. "One thing we promised Noor was that we would get rid of all local accounts everywhere."

"If we integrate all our tools into SSO, it would also help us monitor for any suspicious behavior since we can better correlate user activity," Nigel added.

"That's fine, but I don't want us to get lost in some philosophical discussion about how we need to write more secure code," Boris said, turning back to his computer to continue typing an email.

"Okay. I can see that. I think Zero Trust is about getting rid of trust in digital systems. This means that we have to assume that we're already breached. Like what if the bad guys have already put some malicious code in our systems? Ideally, Zero Trust should help us with that."

"Of course we want to write more secure code, but we're also on a deadline to launch the new treadmills," Boris said as he turned back to look at them directly, crossing his arms again. "There's more hardware-specific code this time because the treadmills have to know what direction you're traveling, but also how fast. One improvement we're expecting later is for the texture of the treadmill to be able to change, like walking on sand or through snow. Or even being able to simulate slipping on ice."

"Remember when we did that OWASP training last year?" Nigel asked. Boris nodded. "I've been thinking about how Zero Trust would really make a difference with those."

"What's OWASP?" Dylan asked.

"OWASP is the Open Web Application Security Project that was started by Mark Curphey and Dennis Groves back in 2001," Nigel said. "At the time, they realized that there were a huge number of vulnerabilities in websites, so they created a project that could give away free resources to developers to help them secure their code."

"What does that have to do with Zero Trust?" Dylan asked.

"OWASP produces a regular list of the most commonly exploited vulnerabilities in web applications. These vulnerabilities all have one thing in common; they all exploit different aspects of trust in digital systems," Nigel said.

"You're right," Boris said.

"Take SQL injection, for example," Nigel said, but seeing Dylan was starting to look lost, he elaborated. "SQL injection happens when an attacker is able to send commands to an interpreter because the developer didn't include proper authentication or input validation. The application should never trust input from a user directly. And queries should be parameterized using prepared statements."

"Go on," Boris said.

"Some applications have issues with broken authentication or broken access controls," Nigel said, trying to catch his breath. "If applications are implemented incorrectly they could expose passwords, keys, or session tokens. Or they could expose other flaws that allow attackers to assume a user's identity. Or if permissions aren't properly enforced inside an application, attackers can exploit those to achieve unauthorized functionality. I've seen programmers just hide things from a user's menu rather than enforce security, and sometimes just viewing the source code on a web page is enough to get access to access other users' accounts, view sensitive files, change access permissions, or even modify other users' data."

"Trust is a vulnerability," Dylan said, echoing what Aaron said when they first met.

Nigel was talking fast now, while Dylan and Boris leaned forward to listen more closely. "Many times I've seen simple misconfigurations of security, or just not configuring security at all and using default configurations, including having open Amazon S3 buckets or using default vendor passwords. Or embedding passwords or other sensitive information inside the code itself. Or exposing sensitive information inside error messages."

"Okay, okay," Boris said. "I see how Zero Trust makes sense when it comes to the most common vulnerabilities. But we're also on a deadline here and we're not getting any additional staff to make our deadlines happen."

"Do we still do automated testing of the code once it hits our CI tool?" Nigel asked.

"Of course, we have to automate testing. That's the cornerstone of DevOps," Boris confirmed.

"What if we put some automated security testing into the CI tool? We could do some light OWASP scanning to make sure that we weren't introducing any delays."

"I don't have any objections to this," Boris said. "Maybe we could do some authentication testing as well. Make sure we're searching for hard-coded data like IP addresses. We'll be introducing some additional enhancements when we release Ben Richards later this month. We should be able to work it in by then," Boris agreed.

"Ben Richards? Isn't that the name of the character Arnold Schwarzenegger played in the movie *The Running Man*?" Dylan asked. "I love that movie."

"Of course. We name all our major builds after famous runners. The last version was codenamed Usain Bolt. The one after Richards is going to be called Florence Griffith-Joyner."

"Flo-Jo? Respect," Dylan said.

"Did we just become best friends?" Boris asked.

"And now you're quoting *Step Brothers*? What is even happening right now?" Dylan said, chuckling.

"Nigel, you didn't tell me Zero Trust was cool. Tell me what else you need to know."

"What about secrets?"

"I've heard that millions of API secret keys are leaked every year because developers wrote them directly into their code. Cybercriminals now scan public repositories and collect those API keys. So we need a way of storing and managing those secret keys that doesn't involve sharing them via email."

"You seem like you might already have something in mind." Boris grinned.

"We should use a scanning tool to detect any API keys or other hard-coded data that's stored in our repositories," Nigel said. "We can use a secret manager to help manage our keys. Rather than hard-coding secrets in our docker ENV files, then sharing them over Slack or Teams, the secret manager will manage those permissions for us."

"Dylan," Boris began, "I'm surprised you haven't asked about our Kubernetes container orchestration system yet."

"What about Kubernetes?" Dylan asked.

"I'm glad you asked. Kubernetes isn't secure at all by default. So we've done a lot already to make sure it's secure. Just like we used to do back when things were all in our data center. We use network segmentation to separate clusters from other workloads and to separate workloads from the Kubernetes control plane. This is only possible if control and data plane traffic are isolated from each other. There should be a firewall between the data and control planes.

"I've also heard that role-based access control isn't enabled by default in Kubernetes. But we can do that now that we're going to integrate with our identity service, right?"

"Yes, this is a lot of work," Boris admitted. "But I actually feel much better about the new product launching now. Not to add more to our plate, but we purchased a tool last year to do runtime security, but we haven't deployed it yet. Is that something you guys can help with?"

"Of course. I'll talk to Isabelle. She'll want some information about the project—can you tell me more about what it does?" Dylan said.

"Since our application runs in the cloud," Boris said, "we've found we actually have less visibility into what the app is doing. I'm worried about container images themselves being compromised before we get them." "But also we need to have a way of figuring out whether our runtime environment is secure so our containers aren't running in privileged mode or getting access to data that a hacker could leverage in a breach. So if our SOC is working the incident response plan, they need to have detailed audit trails of all commands, what files were accessed, and what sessions were in use at what time."

"That's great since we already have it, there won't be any added costs. I think Vic will appreciate that," Dylan said. "We will be meeting with our SOC team soon, but I'll include them in the project."

"What if we can't get to a particular vulnerability for a few weeks? Is there anything that we can do in the meantime to protect our application?" Boris asked.

"At my last job," Dylan said, "we had just completed rolling out a web application firewall or WAF to protect all of our websites. Most WAFs can protect against the most common OWASP attacks or even help detect and prevent credential stuffing attacks where cybercriminals use exposed usernames and passwords from other breaches to break into other services that customers might use."

"We've looked at WAFs before," Nigel said. "The problem was always that they were a proxy. They introduce another single point of failure if they aren't already integrated into our load balancers. And if they aren't integrated with our existing load balancers, then you have to have some manual process to sync certificates around. And the ones that are integrated with our on-premise load balancers won't work with our cloud apps."

"That's true," Dylan said. "But the one we implemented could use an agent on each endpoint. But really, WAFs are just a Band-Aid. We should be including web application testing in our penetration testing schedule to augment our regular testing."

"Dylan, you're really making me think today," Boris said. "One of the pillars of DevOps is the idea of infrastructure as code," Boris said. "We can code instructions on how we expect the environment to work, and then it works without taking weeks or months for a sysadmin to get around to configuring a VM. What if we started thinking of security policies as code as well?"

"Boss, I think you're on to something," Nigel said. "Defining security policies in our code will help us scale up as we roll out features into our different testing and development environments before they go to production. And the security policy code will get checked into our code repositories so it can be versioned, and we can easily recover if something goes wrong."

"What kind of security policies are you thinking about?" Dylan asked.

Nigel was on the edge of his chair now, talking rapidly. "We can define roles and permissions inside code. Enforcing least privilege and separation of duties in code will help keep our developers focused on writing code rather than explaining unique requirements to sysadmins. And it can be audited much more easily since the configurations will be centrally stored rather than being spread across a bunch of different systems."

"This could also help us make sure our developers are never able to log in as root," Boris added. "We've had issues enforcing this in the past. Developers should also be able to assume different roles for testing. Automating this process could really help speed things up."

"One of the things that we are looking for is opportunities to seamlessly inject reauthentications into the process," Dylan said. "Could we also require a new MFA when someone needs to do something major, like pushing new code out?"

"Yes. We can enforce a lot of things in our security policies, like time-of-day access, restricting IP addresses, or requiring SSL connections," Nigel said.

"The final thing that we need to make sure we've got covered is monitoring," Dylan said. "From talking to Noor, we've got our logging pipeline set up for the whole development environment from the code repository to our cloud infrastructure. And when we shift to using identity, this should make it easier for the SOC to correlate events."

"So what else do we need to work on?" Boris asked.

"When is the last time we did a code review?" Dylan asked. "Ideally we should be doing both static and dynamic analysis on a regular schedule like we do for our other penetration testing."

"It's been a couple years," Boris admitted. "But you're right, this is something we should do soon. We don't have a tool that will do this; is that something your penetration testing vendor can help us with?"

"I assume so, but I'll check with them and let you know," Dylan said.

"The last time we did a code review, it didn't really discover anything that we didn't already know about. I honestly couldn't tell if the tool didn't work right or whether the guy running the tool didn't know what he was doing."

"I think we should be taking a belt-and-suspenders approach to testing. I think it's okay to have a couple options on keeping our pants up. Have you ever considered using a bug bounty program?" Dylan asked.

"We proposed this last year," Boris said. "It would take at least three, maybe four developers to manage the program. Half a million to start even before you get to the bounties wasn't going to fly. It got turned down."

"What about the managed bug bounty program companies? They can manage it for us and aren't nearly as expensive," Dylan said.

"We would still need to have someone manage the company and respond to any issues that come in," Boris said, turning to Nigel.

"I'm in. Let's do it!" Nigel said.

"That will help us make the business case. So all our developers have to work on is fixing issues. We can even work with April to make a press release. This could help change the narrative around how MarchFit is responding. I think Vic can get behind that. Making a real difference for security at a fraction of what we thought it would cost in the past."

"How do you want us to engage your team if the pen testers or a bug bounty hunter comes up with an issue?" Dylan asked.

"Well, it has to integrate into our existing process. I don't want our developers to have to log in to the help desk ticket system to look at a bug tracking report," Boris said.

"Boss, I'll be the embedded security liaison into the Zero Trust team," Nigel said. "We'll only engage the team using the same Jira tickets that the team already uses to track other issues."

There was a knock at the door, and Harmony stuck her head into the room. "Hey, boys. Sorry, but I need to talk to Dylan for a second," she said. "Why's it so dark in there? I'm not interrupting anything, am I?"

"Boris is cool," Dylan said. "We don't have any secrets here. You can just tell us."

"Oh, okay," she said, opening the door all the way to let the hallway light in. "We just got a call from our SOC. They're seeing some weird anomalies. Like we're under attack or something. I thought I'd bring you in before I talked to them."

"Is it Encore again?"

"We don't have any way of telling that for sure," she said.

"What, no tweets this time?" Boris joked.

"Nothing on his account. I was hoping it was just scanning, but the logs they sent over look a lot more sophisticated than what we've been seeing from him in the past," she said.

Key Takeaways

Application security is a huge challenge for many organizations. DevOps has revolutionized rapid delivery and continuous improvement of software for organizations; therefore, DevOps can also be an effective partner in delivering Zero Trust. Building Zero Trust into the process itself ensures that security isn't adding additional delays into the application development process.

In this case, the protect surface is the entire DevOps environment, and the transaction flows are all related to the development and deployment process. Often, applications are deployed with service accounts or by developers directly. When identity and access management aren't integrated with the protect surface, each developer may have reused personal usernames or passwords; passwords may not meet complexity requirements; and two-factor authentication may not be enforced. Single Sign On can be a way of reducing the number of logins for users, increasing productivity and improving security.

In some custom applications, developers want to embed identity in the application itself. This should be avoided for a number of reasons. Passwords shouldn't be stored inside your own database. If your app does perform its own authentication, it needs to include a lot of additional custom features, such as password reset or multifactor authentication, that can be better provided by a dedicated identity service. And using a dedicated identity service also ensures that the authenticator for your app stays up to date and secure since in-house resources might get pulled away to maintain other parts of the application.

A big part of integrating Zero Trust into a DevOps environment is integrating with the existing culture of the organization. In the example in this chapter, Nigel is the embedded security team member inside development, but he has been a developer for a number of years and is passionate about bringing security and developers together. The security team will use Jira tickets that the developers already use to be a part of the process. And security testing can be integrated into the testing process as well as at regular intervals.

Traditionally, many of the most common vulnerabilities in the OWASP Top 10 vulnerabilities have been directly attributable to exploiting trust in digital systems. Each year, the OWASP foundation updates the list with the most current attack vectors being seen in the wild.

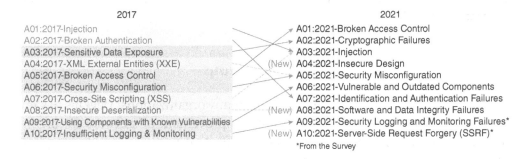

2017	2021
A01:2017-Injection	A01:2021-Broken Access Control
A02:2017-Broken Authentication	A02:2021-Cryptographic Failures
A03:2017-Sensitive Data Exposure	A03:2021-Injection
A04:2017-XML External Entities (XXE)	(New) A04:2021-Insecure Design
A05:2017-Broken Access Control	A05:2021-Security Misconfiguration
A06:2017-Security Misconfiguration	A06:2021-Vulnerable and Outdated Components
A07:2017-Cross-Site Scripting (XSS)	A07:2021-Identification and Authentication Failures
A08:2017-Insecure Deserialization	(New) A08:2021-Software and Data Integrity Failures
A09:2017-Using Components with Known Vulnerabilities	A09:2021-Security Logging and Monitoring Failures*
A10:2017-Insufficient Logging & Monitoring	(New) A10:2021-Server-Side Request Forgery (SSRF)*
	*From the Survey

OWASP Top 10 vulnerabilities
SOURCE: OWASP Top Ten / OWASP Foundation, Inc.

Although Zero Trust doesn't explicitly address techniques to write more secure code, removing the trust relationships around the development process can go a long way toward improving security. Even just removing secrets from being stored in the code directly—like IP addresses, API keys, or passwords—can go a long way toward containing any intrusions. And by integrating with identity services, developer permissions can be limited to only those necessary, further limiting the blast radius of any intrusions.

DevOps is also very focused on using the cloud to rapidly deliver services. Orchestration tools like Kubernetes or Docker can help facilitate scalability, but they also introduce new security challenges that traditional security teams or infrastructure engineers aren't aware of. But there are numerous hardening guides available for these tools, and once you do apply the appropriate security controls, those controls can scale as well.

We don't expect all code to be secure when it enters production. This is where a web application firewall (WAF) can help. WAFs are more aware of applications than traditional firewalls and can do more to protect websites as well. Modern WAFs are able to learn how applications work and can help enforce input validation, detect malicious activity like SQL injection or cross-site scripting or "XSS," and block that activity before it is exploited. But WAFs should only be used as a Band-Aid, so when a vulnerable page or application is found, the underlying vulnerabilities should be fixed as quickly as possible.

DevOps assumes that any issues with code can be rapidly addressed. After a former NSA hacker publicly announced a zero-day vulnerability in Zoom at the beginning of the pandemic in 2020, the company shifted and was able to issue a patch within 24 hours in part because Zoom uses a DevOps development model. DevOps can help improve security rapidly, but the organization needs to be looking for security flaws continuously. Static and dynamic code analysis should be done on a regular basis for all code. Organizations should also host bug bounty programs to help monitor for potential issues and provide the security community with a well-known reporting path for issues.

There is a perception that security is expensive. While there are some fundamental investments that need to be made in security, often security can be done with the tools that the team already has in place. And with DevOps, it's essential to use the tools that developers are already using. Zero Trust can help demonstrate to executives that the organization is pursuing the most effective strategy to secure the organization.

Chapter 7
Zero Trust SOC

Jefferson sat in front of his workstation bleary-eyed from having worked a double shift overnight. He was sitting in front of two curved monitors that almost wrapped around him. The left screen displayed a live stream of logs, filtered by a long search string that Jefferson had painstakingly spent the whole night creating, narrowing the search terms each time he understood a little more about what was going on. On the right screen, his ticket queue was displayed. The more tickets that came in, the more distracted he became. The day crew would start in a few minutes and would help, but he was a little worried his team lead would just dismiss what he had found.

Beyond his monitors was a wall of twelve eighty-inch screens. They showed the weather, news, views of customer networks with colors indicating when they were having issues, and the all-important queue of tickets coming in.

One of the graveyard-shift crew had called in sick. Jefferson didn't have to take the shift. He wasn't on call or anything. But then that would have meant letting go of what he had found. Someone else might not be able to see the pattern of anomalies he had discovered. It was more than just a pattern. He was sure there was coordination behind it.

The only other person on shift was Nadir. Nadir was wearing headphones, but Jefferson could still hear the hair metal music on his side of the room. Jefferson had made the mistake of referring to the music as glam rock at one point and had to listen to a three-hour explanation of the differences between them. As Jefferson was about to work up the courage to ask Nadir for his help, his team lead Luis arrived, several minutes early, carrying enough coffee for both shifts. He took a coffee for himself and set the rest down on the desk next to Jefferson, where everyone else would have to talk to Jefferson. Was that on purpose?

"Thanks for working last night, El Jefe," Luis said, using his nickname for Jefferson. It had started to stick with the rest of the team. Jefferson had only worked in the SOC for a couple months, but somehow that nickname, more than anything else, made him feel like he had a future in cybersecurity. "How'd it go last night?" Luis asked.

Jefferson blinked the sleep out of his eyes, grabbed a coffee, and tried to figure out how to explain everything going through his mind. The coffee tasted like chocolate, with a hint of some nutty flavors he couldn't place. "I've spent the last sixteen hours looking at MarchFit's logs," Jefferson blurted out as he began highlighting logs on his screen to show his findings. "I saw one machine call out to a remote address. The address wasn't on any threat lists, but it had been newly registered in DNS, so I dug a bit further. It was late, so I was pretty sure no one was actually using that computer. I didn't see any other devices connecting to that specific IP. But the fact that there were some low-severity PSExec logs really bothered me."

"How big a problem do you think it is?"

Jefferson didn't know if he should say aloud what he was thinking. Maybe it was because he was so tired. Jefferson had pulled double shifts before and knew how easily confused he got when he hadn't gotten sleep. He blinked as the day-shift analysts came in joking with each other. He leaned in closely to Luis and whispered, "This is 3nc0r3. I know it. I don't know how much longer I can stay awake, but I gotta explain this to someone while I can still talk coherently."

Luis took a long drink of his coffee and tossed the empty cup into the trash. "No problema, Jefe. I'm on it. You get the others up to speed and wait for Money, who will be coming directly."

"You're sending in The Money?" Jefferson exclaimed. "That's all you had to say."

Several minutes later, Harmony led Dylan down the stairs into MarchFit's basement. At the bottom was an old-style freight elevator with a sliding fence for a door. There were rows of chain link fencing around the basement making up storage areas for different departments. The lighting was terrible, but Dylan noticed cages full of treadmills, and cages full of returned merchandise, alongside cages full of old, clearly broken computer equipment. They turned right where a row of cages ended, dim light leaking in from a tiny window.

"How does the SOC know if a device has multiple IP addresses?" Dylan asked. "Do they think that those are two different devices? Or do they have a way of resolving those devices into a single entity?"

"They don't know," Harmony answered. "They can see our DHCP logs, but we have to resolve devices in our inventory system after they alert us."

"What about identities? Do they have a way of looking at a user and finding all the devices they've interacted with?" Dylan asked.

"Again, no." Harmony pulled a chain and a row of incandescent bulbs started to blink on, illuminating the rest of the basement in a harsh white light. "We've got some tools internally that have this, but the SOC doesn't have access to them."

"How do they know when one of our tools finds something potentially malicious?" Dylan asked.

"The tools send an alert to the SIEM, and they will see that in the logs," Harmony said.

"But if they don't have access to our internal security tools, how can they do investigations into what is going on?" Dylan asked.

"They can't," Harmony said.

"So all they can do is see an alert in our logging system, and the only thing they can do is tell us about it so we can go investigate ourselves?" Dylan stopped to look at some old servers that were stacked on a pallet wrapped in plastic like they were ready to be recycled. He was pleased to note that the hard drive bays had all been removed. Those must be somewhere else, hopefully being erased. He'd have to ask about that.

"Don't our tools have APIs that they can connect to?" Harmony suggested. "That could give them access to the data without giving them direct access to those systems. Would that accomplish the goal of having Zero Trust?"

"I've heard of some places that also monitor access to APIs. We should look into that soon," Dylan said. "But you're right, I bet someday all logs will be sent over APIs."

"This is us," Harmony said, going through a rusted door into another darkened room. A sign written on a piece of torn poster board above the door read "Abandon All Trusts, Ye Who Enter."

"Um, where are you taking me again?" Dylan asked as he entered. The only light came from numerous computer monitors around the room, haphazardly hung on the walls or arranged on the makeshift table in the center of the room made up of old doors that had been taken off their hinges. "This reminds me of a movie. *Johnny Mnemonic*, I think," he said.

"That's exactly the look I was going for!" Harmony said, taking her spot in a chair that looked like it was salvaged from a racing car. "Sit next to me so we can both see their screen," she said as she began the Zoom call. Dylan sat down in the chair next to her. It had also been salvaged from the junk pile, apparently. He looked around the room. There was a poster featuring the actor David Duchovny from *X-Files* across from them that read "Trust No One." He had the distinct impression that he was in Harmony's personal man cave. Woman cave? Or was it a she-shed?

"Thanks for waiting, guys," Harmony said. "Thought my new boss would want to hear what you had to say. What's up, Jefe, you look like crud. You been up all night?"

Jefferson and Luis were both on the Zoom, along with two other members of the SOC.

After several seconds, Jefferson realized they were talking to him. "You guys know what PSExec is? Right?" Not waiting for an answer, he continued, "It's this utility that lets you run commands remotely so long as File and Printer Sharing is enabled on your target and you have credentials on your target?"

"Right," Harmony said.

Jefferson was talking rapidly between sips of coffee. "I had just finished this course on PowerShell, but we already have detections for that in our platform. So I started doing some threat hunting in our customer base to see if we saw any PSExec activity similar to what we would normally look for in PowerShell. And it turns out one of your machines was showing activity after the user had left for the day. The script was just dumping hardware info, so it didn't rise to a critical-level alert, but I knew Money would want to know about that kind of thing, so I kept looking at it."

Dylan grabbed the mouse and muted the Zoom meeting. "Did that guy just call you Money?"

"Yeah, it's embarrassing," Harmony said. "But it's kinda sweet, so I never said anything."

"Do they even know your real name?" Dylan asked, noticing that she had changed her Zoom profile name to #Money.

"Probably?" she said. "Shush, this was just getting interesting," she said and unmuted.

"Later on, I saw some EDR alerts for the same system that there were some blocked attempts to run a crypto mining installer. This didn't rise to the level of a critical alert because the attempt was blocked. But there were more until I saw that a cryptominer was successfully installed and we escalated. I think the bad guys were dumping hardware info to see what cryptominer would work best on that system before they actually installed it."

"Where were the attempts coming from?" Dylan asked.

"This user was working from home and the requests were coming from another device on the local network."

"Thanks, Jefe, " Harmony said. "Dylan, what do you think the chances are for us to get Noor's approval to disable File and Printer Sharing?"

"I'll ask," Dylan said, typing an instant message to Noor asking her to join the call. "But I'm wondering about whether our SOC is another protect surface we need to work on."

"Boss, you might be on to something," Harmony said.

Dylan noticed the Zoom alert at the top of the screen showing that Noor was requesting to enter the meeting. After getting Noor up to speed, she asked, "I assume we've removed the cryptominer?"

Luis nodded and said, "Yes. We sent a ticket to your help desk when we first reached out to Harmony and just got the response that the ticket has been closed."

"Thank you all for your dedicated work. I love to see that kind of initiative," Noor said. "But I'm a little worried about whether we can scale our response when we have so many users. How do we respond faster next time?"

"I think I can help with that," said one of the other individuals from the SOC. "Sorry for not introducing myself earlier, I didn't want to interrupt our analyst while he was giving you the update. I'm Chris Grey, I'm the owner of the MSSP and I've been hearing a lot about your Zero Trust implementation and wanted to learn more. So it's good timing for a conversation."

"What have you heard?" Dylan asked.

"We've seen the number of alerts start to go down dramatically over the last month or so from MarchFit. Which is really interesting, because at the same time the volume of logs you've been sending to us has gone way up," Chris said.

"That is interesting," Dylan said. "I know it's hard to detect some of these issues since you guys don't know everything about how the business functions. We need you to be more of a design partner for a Zero Trust focused service."

"From my perspective," Chris said, "we don't have a detection problem in the SOC. We have a response problem. Our whole model is designed around providing as much detection as possible, logging everything, but it's up to someone else to figure out whether it matters. We don't have parsers built for all the new application-specific logs we're getting from you now, for example. We need to understand Zero Trust more from you. I like the idea of building a SOC around Zero Trust."

"We'd love to hear your ideas," Noor said.

"We've got a basic partnership today, sending tickets that MarchFit has to respond to," Chris began. "But to be successful, we need to be involved with incident response as well, and we can help automate the response."

"Wait, will this cost more?" Dylan asked.

"We're still developing our managed response service, but I think if we can do this right, it should actually reduce the costs of the service because it takes less effort. With our playbook, we have automated responses already developed for the known bad things out there. Usually the known bad things out there can be blocked. It's the unknown malicious activity we need to respond to. But what gets in the way is all of the noise. The false positives. If we can eliminate 99 percent of all the false positives, then what's left will be much easier to investigate and act upon. But we need to be aligned with what you're doing on Project Zero Trust to make sure we're keeping up."

"If we're going to start a Zero Trust partnership with the SOC," Dylan said, "let's go back to basics. Harmony, can you pull up the design principles?"

Harmony shared her screen, showing the four Zero Trust design principles:

1. Focus on business outcomes.
2. Design from the inside out.
3. Determine who/what needs access.
4. Inspect and log all traffic.

"The first part of Zero Trust is about knowing the business," Dylan explained. "How we make money, what the strategy is, and where the business plans to go."

"So what does that mean for MarchFit?" Chris asked.

"We have several lines of business," Dylan said. "We have our retail outlets. But we also have our network of content creators that people love taking walks or runs with. And then there is our new product development that is launching a new product in a few months."

"I think we can better align with MarchFit's Zero Trust implementation by customizing our runbooks around those different lines of business," Chris offered. "I bet that each of those different lines of business rely on different business-critical applications, and we can tailor our monitoring to more closely mirror that first design principle. What about being inside out?"

"That has defined our approach," Dylan said. "We've prioritized working on our most business-critical protect surfaces first, and then expanded from there."

Chris nodded. "That makes sense. Instead of putting all your controls at the perimeter firewall, you're doing that crunchy center thing that John Kindervag talked about. It seems like we should be able to align our monitoring around those protect surfaces as they relate to those different lines of business."

"How does the SOC know who or what needs access?" Harmony asked.

"We've recently built our own security orchestration system to help automate the runbook actions that we're able to take," Chris said. "To be successful at this, we'd need to be able to integrate with your identity system. We use our orchestration platform to help establish behavioral norms. A behavior that's normal in one region or one department might be a critical alert if it's discovered in a different region or department. That's our secret sauce."

"The costs of logging everything might be too high to include our MSSP in step 4," Noor said. "Storage costs are going down all the time, but you have to admit that there's a disincentive to send everything to our MSSP since you charge based on the volume of logs. You're not charging based on how effective your service is."

"If we're not providing value, then we would expect you to leave and find another MSSP," Chris admitted. "And I also understand that we weren't able to detect most of the activity that led up to your ransomware infection. We need to do better, not just for you, but for all our clients. I agree that we need to have some skin in the game. But we also need a feedback loop to help MarchFit improve your controls. The more false positives we can remove by stopping bad behavior, the more time we can spend investigating real suspicious activity."

"There are also five design principles that we're following," Harmony said, advancing to the next slide:

1. Define the protect surface.
2. Map the transaction flows.
3. Architect a Zero Trust environment.
4. Create Zero Trust policies.
5. Monitor and maintain each protect surface.

"I see that step five is to monitor and maintain each protect surface," Chris said. "I think we can align our controls around your defined protect surfaces. This will help us provide better monitoring, but it will also allow us to provide better feedback on what is slipping through your controls. Or in Zero Trust terminology, we can help look for opportunities to remove trust from these different protect surfaces."

Noor folded her arms, looking away from the screen for a moment. "How does the SOC keep up with all the changes that are going on in our environment?"

"The only way that we can scale is for the SOC to be the nerve center of security. Your logs will provide the baseline. We'll also need to have API access to your inventory and vulnerability management systems in order to enrich this data so that we know in real time as the transaction flows change over time or when devices are patched or updated. Just like Shift Left philosophy has led developers to get involved earlier in the process, we've applied the Shift Left approach to our SOC. The goal will be to move people like Jefferson away from simply looking through logs and alerts to writing scripts and building new orchestrations."

"Is there a way that you can be involved in architecture?" Dylan asked.

"We use MITRE's ATT&CK framework to help provide context to our analysts on what a particular action means in a given situation," Chris said. "The ATT&CK framework helps provide context to why a particular action is being taken and helps predict what actions might come next. There is actually a finite list of threat actors out there, and many of them use similar tactics, techniques, and practices, or TTPs. Just like one of your engineers might be an expert on a particular Microsoft product, so too attackers become familiar with a small set of techniques and they'll try to leverage those skills against the same vulnerabilities over and over again."

"How does that help?" Harmony asked.

"With our orchestration system, we've developed runbooks for these common attacks. For example, we have orchestrations for PowerShell, domain admin, or VPN compromises. And we also define what good behavior looks like. As we see bad behavior, we should be able to provide recommendations on additional controls, firewall rules, or config changes that could block those TTPs moving forward."

"I'm still not sure if we're really doing Zero Trust here," Dylan said. "Zero Trust is all about prevention. What we're talking about is reactive instead of being proactive."

Harmony interrupted. "Didn't Aaron say that Zero Trust is about containing breaches?"

Dylan nodded. "Everything we've done so far has contained the breach to a specific protect surface," he said. "I agree that we need to have continuous improvement, but I don't know if we're really aligning with Zero Trust principles here."

"If I'm understanding you correctly, containment doesn't just happen in a protect surface. What we're doing in our SOC is helping to reduce the time that an attacker is inside your network. We know that this dwell time in some instances can be hundreds of days. If we can contain an attack in terms of duration, then aren't we still on the right track with Zero Trust?"

"That makes sense," Dylan admitted.

"I don't want to make it seem like there's a conflict of interest in giving you advice," Chris said. "So you can feel free to buy additional tools or service from whoever you want to work with. But as your SOC, we want to help you find your blind spots."

"What do you mean by blind spots?" Noor asked.

"Sometimes we'll send alerts when we see a server stop sending logs," Jefferson said. "A silent log source could mean the server has crashed or has been compromised and you might not know about it."

Chris nodded. "Another example could be network-based detection. While we definitely need server logs, that only gives us part of the picture. There are several good network detection and response, or NDR, tools out there, but you can also use the open source tool Zeek to provide network logs. We also know that ninety-eight percent of all network traffic is now encrypted, so decryption might be appropriate in some cases, or else we may need to find a solution that provides insight through analyzing headers. If you can enrich those network logs with proactive threat hunting, you not only remove a blind spot, but you improve your vision as well. Some of our clients have been able to detect whether some recent critical zero-day vulnerabilities were present in their networks or confirm for sure that they weren't impacted by a vulnerability because they had an NDR platform."

"I think I'm starting to see why monitor and maintain is such an important part of the process," Harmony said. "I wish we had been more focused on this stage from the beginning."

"There are other examples as well," Chris added. "Jefferson's point about blind spots can also extend to cloud logging where you may not have the same visibility. Having a cloud access security broker, or CASB, can give you a similar increase in visibility. We also offer penetration testing, for example. Whether you use us for penetration testing or whether you have another vendor for that, I think we should share the results of the test with our SOC to help understand the environment. Same thing with your regular vulnerability scans. We can enrich our inventory and provide more customized runbooks for you."

"You mentioned that you have an orchestration system," Dylan said. "How does that part work?"

"We know it takes several minutes for even the best-trained analysts to review an alert and decide how to respond. With the volume of attacks that are happening, we want to reduce response time down to seconds. We know the attackers have automated their attacks, so the only way to keep up is to have a machine respond in real time," Chris said.

"What happens if we accidentally disable an important service with an automated rule?" Noor asked.

"I completely understand your concern," Chris said. "What some of our clients do is to have us monitor core services or provide access to your monitoring tools. We can also orchestrate a fallback in cases where we detect that a service has been disrupted. But we are in an age where we can't risk testing patches for months before moving to production. We've monitored this over time and patching has become less disruptive than it was ten years ago. Many of our clients have told us that it's less risky overall to patch first and then test afterward so that you've reduced your exposure."

"So you're saying it's risky to be proactive, but it's more risky to be reactive?" Dylan asked.

Chris chuckled. "There are ways to be proactive without being risky. We have clients that have supplemented their controls with deception technologies like honeypots or honeytokens. I don't recommend making a honeypot device accessible to the public Internet. But if you do deploy those internally, they can be an early warning system to detect when an attacker has gotten past your defenses. For example, we know that as a part of the reconnaissance step in the ATT&CK framework, threat actors will enumerate all your public-facing server certificates and then target those servers. Putting a fake certificate there for an internal honeypot server can help you disrupt the initial access stage of attacks. The NSA has tested this, and they've shown that attackers spend less time in networks when deception tools are deployed."

"That brings up another issue," Harmony said. "I've been on our monthly SOC briefings in the past and I think we can step up our game when it comes to reporting. Is there a way we can measure how effective we are at containment? We don't want reporting that says you responded to tickets within five minutes or how many cases you opened. That doesn't tell us that we're more secure or more effective. If we're going to have a Zero Trust SOC, we want to report on how many false positives we've reduced. I'd like to know many new rules you have added to your runbook and how many of them have been applied in our environment. How does that compare to the previous month? And how does it compare to the same time the previous year since we may have seasonal changes. Does it look like attacks are advancing through the MITRE ATT&CK framework and are we being successful at disrupting the later stages like command and control?"

"I was thinking we should have weekly briefings instead of monthly," Chris added. "But I agree we should provide better insights to align with your Zero Trust strategy."

"OK, I think we're on the same page," Noor said. "I've got to run to another meeting, but I'd like to have our Zero Trust team schedule another meeting to make sure you're in the loop on all of our progress so far."

The wind was blowing heavily as Dylan walked one of the running paths that circled the building. He pressed the dial button for Aaron's number. It rang four times before Aaron answered.

"Calling already?" Aaron asked. "Everything OK?"

"Sorry for bugging you, but I wanted to ask about our SOC. We're aligning our Zero Trust processes with their monitoring. I wanted to make sure I wasn't missing anything."

"It's critical that they can provide feedback to you on what controls are working and how you can improve. But have you asked yourself what happens after the SOC finds something?"

"What do you mean?" Dylan asked.

"The SOC is another protect surface," Aaron said. "You need to incorporate Zero Trust into the incident response process itself. The incident response process is the main way that you'll interact with a SOC."

"Really?" Dylan asked. "You think we can do Zero Trust in the incident response process?"

"I definitely think Zero Trust applies to the incident response process. Managed Security Service Providers are a critical partner, but they're a huge target for attackers because they have connectivity inside the most sensitive parts of hundreds or thousands of customer networks. This is true for any IT service. Two-thirds of breaches come from your vendors. If you haven't started looking at third-party vendor management, you might add that to the list, particularly for cloud service providers."

"What do you mean?"

"Sorry, gotta run," Aaron interrupted, and hung up.

The Zero Trust team was waiting for Dylan in Harmony's basement command center. Someone had found a lamp so the room actually had some light this time. Isabelle was speaking with Rose as both examined Isabelle's tablet. There were more chairs now, but Brent and Nigel were standing together in the corner. Jefferson and Luis were on Zoom, but their images were now being projected onto a screen strapped with zip ties to the dropped ceiling, the ceiling tiles no longer sitting flush with the ceiling.

"We haven't talked yet about what happens after an incident," Dylan began. "Up until now, other teams have been engaged with the incident response process and we've been focused on hardening other protect surfaces. The SOC and the incident response process is another protect surface."

"In our SOC," Luis began, "we've aligned our controls around the NIST Cyber-security Framework since most of our clients are already using that to measure the maturity of their security programs."

"Sorry. Wait, how many NIST standards are there?" Brent asked. "I thought there was just the one for Zero Trust?"

"Thousands," Dylan said. "They make standards about almost everything. It helps support the economy by making businesses more efficient, and consequently more competitive."

Luis shared his screen and displayed a picture showing the five steps of the NIST Cybersecurity Framework:

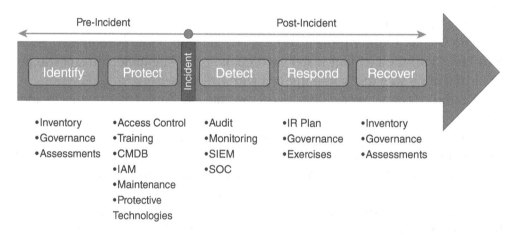

NIST Cybersecurity Framework
SOURCE: Adapted from NIST Cybersecurity framework

"The NIST Cybersecurity Framework is a five-step process to help organizations ensure that they've put adequate controls in place to organize their resources and protect themselves from cybercriminals," Luis explained. "The framework is organized into a timeline around the assumption that the organization will be breached. The first two functions in the process, Identify and Protect, both happen before an incident happens. The final three functions, Detect, Respond, and Recover, all happen after an incident occurs. The other NIST security control publications like Special Publication 800-53 for government entities or 800-171 for nongovernment entities or even ISO 27001 or the CSC top twenty controls can all be mapped to the five-step framework."

"Since Zero Trust is all about prevention, doesn't it only apply to the first two steps?" Brent asked.

"It's true that Zero Trust focuses on prevention," Dylan said. "And the model we use for helping us remove trust is by assuming we've already been breached. The whole reason that we send our logs to a centralized logging system is that we expect that the first thing a cybercriminal will do is try to remove any logs or other evidence of their activity. Zero Trust definitely continues after an incident occurs."

"We based our incident response plan on the NIST SP 800-61," Harmony said to Brent as she pointed to the screen. "It goes into more detail on the final three steps of the Cybersecurity Framework. It's a little older than the Cybersecurity Framework, so it uses some slightly different terminology. But NIST makes standards for everything. They've been around for a hundred years."

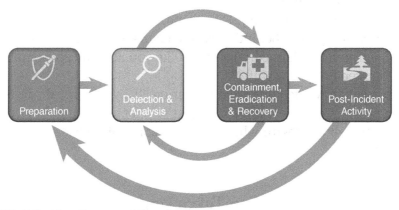

NIST SP 800-61 Incident Response Lifecycle
SOURCE: P Cichonski et al., (2012)/NIST/Public domain

"If a computer is compromised," Dylan began, "we definitely won't trust it. But we've also got to decide whether we power it off or take it off the network. Do we monitor the compromised computer to see what other devices it may be connecting to?"

"In the incident response process, what we're talking about is the containment, eradication, and recovery stage," Luis responded. "We'd need to consider several factors, including potential damage that could be caused or whether theft of data is likely to occur. Do we need to preserve any evidence? Would taking down a system impact a critical service? Do we have the time and resources to respond adequately? Do we need full containment? Or will partial containment be enough? And are we implementing an emergency workaround? Because sometimes emergency workarounds end up being there for years afterward."

"All right," Dylan said. "Let's start by reviewing our incident response plan. If the SOC is our protect surface, then the plan will be our map of transaction flows. Our CMDB and disaster recovery tools are the architecture. And the CISRT team will be the ones who need access. We'll begin a weekly SOC meeting to monitor the alignment of Project Zero Trust controls with how the SOC monitors the organization. What else are we missing?"

"We should do a practice fire drill before the product launch to make sure all of our processes are working correctly," Isabelle said.

"You mean a tabletop exercise?" Dylan said.

"Exactly," Isabelle said. "Can we hire a company to hack us as a part of the exercise? Make it a real test."

"That does sound interesting," Dylan said.

Another person walked behind Luis and handed him a paper. It was Jefferson.

"Jefe!" Harmony exclaimed. "You look like you actually got some sleep! Did you get promoted to the day shift?"

Jefferson bent down to join the conversation. "Hey, guys, yeah, day shift now! Sorry to interrupt. Our threat intel team just sent a note saying they've found an open Amazon S3 bucket with what looks like some of your data. Can you guys take a look?"

Key Takeaways

Alert fatigue is a real thing. A medium-sized company might produce millions of logs per day. A large organization might produce billions. Separating all the logs generated from normal activity from the tiny number of logs generated by a malicious actor is like finding a needle in a haystack. Many of the alerts that are generated are false positives, and this desensitizes the analyst performing the detective work. There are ways of mitigating this desensitization, but the most effective approach is to reduce or remove the noise that causes alert fatigue in the first place. Zero Trust can help with this, but only if the SOC is a part of your Zero Trust journey.

As Chris indicated, the SOC doesn't have a problem detecting issues; they have a response problem. How do you separate out all the noise and false positives and end up with actionable information that allows you to respond to a threat actor in real time? This takes very mature playbooks, teams of well-trained threat hunters, and automation capabilities. But it also takes the insights and lessons learned from monitoring attackers and the tactics, techniques, and procedures (TTPs) they leverage against not just from a single company but from hundreds or thousands of other organizations.

For this reason, many organizations choose to outsource their SOC to a third-party Managed Security Service Provider (MSSP). An MSSP can provide real value in terms of maturing a cybersecurity program, but there are many challenges to overcome. MSSPs need to be able to support clients in many different industries using many different types of software. To be successful in this role, MSSPs need to be able to understand how your business works, what your crown jewels are, and what users are allowed to have access to. When a company is on its Zero Trust journey, the MSSP should be more than a participant—they should be a partner.

The final design principle of Zero Trust is to inspect and log all traffic. The final step in the Zero Trust design methodology is to monitor and maintain each protect surface. Implicit in both these directives is the notion that someone is analyzing the information being gathered from the environment and learning from it. There should be a feedback loop from the SOC to the organization on what potential vulnerabilities are being targeted and what changes can be made to better defend your protect surfaces. And based on their knowledge of how threat actors are targeting other similar organizations, they should be able to help you identify where your own blind spots are and where any potential deficiencies in tooling or configuration may be.

In other words, to be successful, an MSSP needs to have skin in the game. An MSSP needs to be able to help influence the organization to proactively update its defenses. The goal of an MSSP is to help enable an organization to reduce the dwell time of an attacker, which is another way of containing an attacker.

To help provide a measure of containment, a SOC should report using a framework that shows how an organization is disrupting attackers' operations. The MITRE ATT&CK framework is the leading knowledge base of attacker tactics, techniques, and processes. This framework can provide needed context to organizations to understand what an attacker is doing and what they might do next. This context is critical in helping contain and reduce dwell time of attackers.

The primary way that a SOC will interact with an organization is through its incident response (IR) process. Many MSSPs offer a variety of services, and an IR response can be as little as sending a company an email when the SOC has observed some suspicious behavior to completely managing the quarantine and patching of an infected device. The more that the SOC can be engaged to support a client, the better the analysis that Zero Trust principles require. To reinforce the client's Zero Trust journey, the SOC should align its monitoring around the client's Zero Trust protect surfaces to better apply that analysis toward improving controls.

The NIST Cybersecurity Framework defines five core functions that all organizations need to be able to accomplish to have a complete cybersecurity program: identify, protect, detect, respond, and recover. These functions align with a timeline around a data breach, so that after the protect stage, you need to plan for what you will do after some malicious activity happens. You should be able to detect when something bad happens, then respond to it, and then recover your business to the place it was before an incident. The SOC will help you perform all three of those final functions.

Almost every cybersecurity program in the United States will be expected to align with the NIST Cybersecurity Framework. The NIST Computer Security Incident Handling Guide (Special Publication 800-61) is the specific standard for how incident response plans should be written. Incident response plans should be tested and updated regularly against real-world scenarios to ensure that they meet the needs of the business.

Chapter 8
Cloudy with a Chance of Trust

Rose's cheek was pressed into the mat. Her opponent, Mark, was sitting on her back, elbow pressing against her head and holding her down. Everything in her screamed to tap out. Instead, she rolled to her side while she pulled her legs up to her chest into a fetal position, breaking the hold. At the same time, she slammed her elbow into Mark's ribs. She followed this by grabbing his wrist and twisted until she wrapped her legs around his arm. He groaned as she followed with several rabbit punches into the same rib that she'd found with her elbow until she realized he was slapping the mat with his free hand. Reluctantly, she let go of him.

She stood up and retied the belt of her gi that had come undone as she had been pinned. She bumped fists with Mark. There weren't many women at the gym and usually the men didn't want to fight for fear of hurting her, or worse, getting beaten by her. Maybe she'd have to let him win next time to keep from running out of sparring partners. She wondered about that as she walked back to grab her water and check her phone. She saw she had missed several calls and texts, but didn't recognize the numbers. She had to brush her hair out of her face before she could get the facial recognition to work.

She dropped the phone when she read the last message. "This is 3nc0r3. I know who you are and I will pay $5 million for information about Zero Trust at MarchFit."

Back at the office, Dylan checked the meeting invite on his phone for the third time. It said "Conference Room 217." He double-checked the room number, but the door was closed so he didn't want to interrupt another meeting. He could hear people talking in the room, so he hesitated for a moment before going in.

Dylan couldn't see through the glass wall of the conference room. It was completely covered by hundreds of Post-it notes. He heard Isabelle's voice and decided it was OK to go in. As he entered the room, he realized that it wasn't just one wall, but all of the walls were covered in Post-it notes. The notes went from one color to another as they wrapped around the room. Isabelle was at the far end of the room writing a note with a Sharpie. There were two other people in the room; both looked up as Dylan entered.

"Is this a prank or something?" Dylan chuckled. He realized the whole surface of the conference room table was also completely covered.

"Oh, good—you're here," Isabelle said, looking at her watch. "You know Kofi already, and this is Dave," she said, pointing to the two other attendees. They stood up to shake Dylan's hand.

"I've been thinking about the cloud," Isabelle said.

"This whole open S3 bucket thing has been bothering me, too," Dylan admitted. "We've confirmed that there wasn't any sensitive information in it, but I'm not sure how we keep up with every new issue out there before they come back to bite us. It seems like there are a handful of common mistakes we're making with our cloud services. The cloud is just too big a protect surface for me to wrap my mind around."

"I've been wondering about that," Isabelle said. "I don't think the cloud is a protect surface."

"What do you mean?" Dylan asked.

"It's a lot of different protect surfaces. Like you said, they all have similar issues that we need to address. I took all the different projects we've worked on over the last couple years. There would have been a lot of opportunities for us to review security best practices at the beginning of a project. Where do you want me to start?"

"Did Harmony get you the list of cloud apps?" Dylan asked.

"Yes. She ran a report from our firewall that showed all traffic going to the most common cloud applications," Isabelle confirmed. "It included some of the apps we expected, like Office365. But there was also a lot of traffic going to unsanctioned cloud applications."

"Like what?" Dylan asked.

"We officially support OneDrive as our online file storage. But we still see traffic going to Dropbox, for example. It's hard to tell at this point whether they're being used for a specific business reason or for personal things," Isabelle said.

"Shouldn't we just block the ones we don't know about?" Kofi asked.

"We always want to be careful. I know our content creators who film themselves taking walks through parks or on beaches upload videos to Vimeo for our production staff to approve before going into production. But I happen to know of cases where one of our most famous creators likes to upload them to YouTube or Twitch where they have other followers, so we wouldn't want to break a business process without understanding the business first. That's the first principle of Zero Trust. But there were other apps being used, like free online PDF converters, which made me start thinking about shadow IT. I started thinking about whether there was another way of tracking down some of those other apps."

"That's why Dave is here," Isabelle said. "He's our head of purchasing."

"I reviewed our purchases for the last year, and all of the Post-its with stars on them are ones we found that were paid by a purchasing card," Dave said. There were a lot of stars up on the wall. "We know there are probably some that are free or trial versions."

"We also can't see what all the people working from home are using," Dylan said. "That could be a blind spot for us."

"That bothers me," Kofi said. "All of those services have terms and conditions that people are clicking through. This list will be very helpful when we review our contracts to make sure we're not opening ourselves to risks."

"Well, let's start with the ones we have. It looks like you guys have already gotten us off to a great start. Let's focus on the applications that may have sensitive info," Dylan said.

"We should definitely focus on those as their own protect surfaces. But I was actually wondering if the protect surface we should be focusing on is actually our project management process," Isabelle said.

"What makes you say that?" Dylan asked.

"There are a lot of things that we need to do every time we bring in a new vendor. The cloud is just another way of saying we're outsourcing a service to another company. But if we don't have a process to make sure our vendors are secure before we onboard them, then we're setting ourselves up to fail," Isabelle said.

Dylan looked around at all the Post-it notes. He realized that the different colors of Post-it notes actually represented the different categories of vendors. Yellow roughly corresponded to the services running on Amazon. Blue notes were Microsoft Azure. Pink were various SaaS services. "So if the protect surface is project management, then mapping the transaction flows is really about understanding the contract process?" he wondered aloud.

"Exactly," Isabelle said. "We've done a lot of work getting different departments to work with us earlier so that we're not surprised when a new request comes in. And it's helped us reduce the amount of shadow IT. But we need help from legal, which is why I invited Kofi to join us."

"We follow three different processes for contracts," Kofi began. "Most contracts go through our purchase order process. We include some standard terms in every PO, including some basic security language. Some other organizations will want us to sign their contract, and we will negotiate our standard terms and conditions into each contract. This can take some time depending on how complex the negotiation is and how much the vendor charges."

"You said there were three options?" Dylan asked.

"In some cases, a vendor will agree to use our standard contract. That's the easiest," Kofi said.

"What do our standard contract terms say?" Dylan asked.

"We ask every vendor to commit to having insurance, encrypting sensitive data, paying the costs of a data breach, and that they have security monitoring in place and perform annual audits," Kofi said." If something happens, we ask them to pay the costs of breach notifications. And if there is a data breach, we indicate that this is a breach of contract and we can get out of the agreement if we need to."

"That all sounds good," Dylan admitted. "Do we just take vendors at their word? Or do we validate that they have security controls in place?"

"At my last company we had a staff of fifteen individuals who would go out and audit our most important vendors," Kofi said. "But I know this isn't feasible for us. I've heard that there are several security vendors that track companies' cybersecurity ratings similar to how the credit ratings agencies track your credit score. I've been thinking that we should use one of those services to monitor our vendors instead of having our own internal team that audits. We can also supplement this with an industry security questionnaire like the one for Shared Assessments Standard Information Gathering, or SIG, and compare their answers with their vendor scorecard."

"That's a great start, Kofi," Dylan said. "I know the Cloud Security Alliance has their Security Trust Assurance and Trust registry as well. We can search through that to see each vendor's Consensus Assessments Initiative Questionnaire, or CIAQ, as well. That could help us see if any of the vendors on the list have any issues. But I'm also worried about how much visibility we're losing when we're outsourcing to the cloud. Most of the data that our SOC collects is from servers or network traffic. Most of our applications are SaaS based, and that means we're not getting much data from those other vendors."

"What about a CASB?" Dave asked. Everyone turned to stare at him.

"What's a CASB?" Isabelle asked.

"It's a cloud access security broker," Dave said. "I did an RFP for a CASB project at my last company. For some of our applications, it acted as a cloud-based proxy. Since all of our traffic was flowing through that, we could collect logs from it. And we customized it for some critical applications to be able to do more specific activity monitoring."

"That was just for some applications?" Dylan asked.

"The CASB also had APIs developed for some of the more popular applications out there like SharePoint or OneDrive," Dave said. "Those were easy to turn on since there was no proxy to configure. And those had a lot more detail already built in for activity monitoring. It was also a great way to detect sensitive information being stored in the cloud."

"Wait," Isabelle said, going back to her tablet. "CASB sounds familiar. We had a project request for this last year. The scope of the project was just for one file-sharing application. But the project was abandoned after the company switched to another tool. But I bet we're still licensed for it."

"Can you ask Noor for help prioritizing the list?" Dylan asked. "Let's focus on the highest-risk SaaS services to secure first. I would think that online file storage should be one of the first since there's probably some sensitive data shared on those apps for teams to work on. Same with SharePoint, Jira, Zoom, or Slack."

"It's getting late, but I'll follow up with her tomorrow," Isabelle said.

"Let's get back to your original point, Isabelle," Dylan said. "I think the project process is a great way to enforce some security standards across the board. We can include phase-gates in the process where we separate a project into phases that are separated by a decision point. The CIO or a governance group could then decide to proceed with subsequent phases or not."

"What kinds of protections should we be looking for?" Dave asked.

"Obviously we want to check for any unsecured cloud storage containers, like the open Amazon S3 bucket we found. Our SOC is now regularly checking for this, but it would be better if we secured them before a project went live."

"That makes sense," Dave said. "What else?"

"First, we should start with making sure those applications are automatically set to be patched," Dylan said. "We need to require MFA for all applications. And we should know whether they support full MFA or just SMS. We should deploy a WAF to all our cloud apps if we can. Make sure insecure ports like telnet are disabled. And the SOC should be aware of applications coming online so they can monitor for any remote access attempts."

"What about error pages?" Isabelle asked.

"Error pages?" Dylan asked.

"I've heard error pages can sometimes leak information," Isabelle said. "I heard from one project manager that their AWS install keys were being leaked by an error message in one of their pages. That allowed an attacker to create their own crypto mining servers using that key. At the end of the month they got a huge bill for those services."

Dylan looked at the Post-it notes across the glass wall. He could see people walking down the hallway passing behind the blue Microsoft Azure columns of Post-it notes, then passing behind the orange Amazon Post-its, then on to the pink SaaS notes. They stopped, turned, and went back as though they had forgotten something, passing behind all those Post-its again.

"There's a lot of interaction among all these services, isn't there?" Dylan wondered. Isabelle, Dave, and Kofi all looked at the board where he was looking. "We're talking about visibility and control for users as they interact with these apps. But I think we're still missing something—the people."

Twenty minutes after the meeting had ended, Dylan was alone in the conference room, still looking at the Post-its. He pressed the button on his cell to call Aaron and explained what they were doing. They needed to be able to enforce policy across all their apps and all their various cloud providers. And they needed to be able to manage policies across all of those different apps. Aaron listened politely for a few minutes, then interrupted. "Software-defined perimeter."

"Software-defined perimeter?" Dylan asked.

"Yes. SDP for short," Aaron confirmed.

"I thought the whole point of Zero Trust was to get rid of the perimeter concept?" Dylan asked.

"Well, yes, you got me there. I wasn't the marketing guy who thought up the acronym, though. You ran across the concept already, inside NIST 800-207. It was called a policy engine. Here, let me text you a picture of what I mean."

Dylan switched to speakerphone and opened the picture.

"The policy enforcement point, in this case, is just an agent on the client that connects back to the policy engine to allow or deny activity based on that employee's role," Aaron explained.

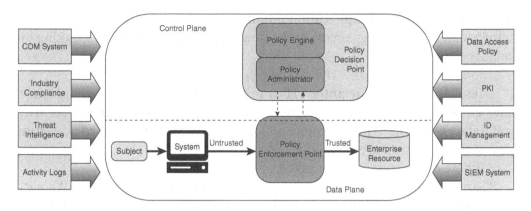

NIST SP 800-207 Core Zero Trust logical components

"That's how we're supposed to manage all our cloud services sprawl?" Dylan asked. "With SDP?"

"It's still the wild west out there," Aaron admitted. "There are a lot of ways to do SDP. But the best approach I've seen uses another acronym, SASE or SSE. Secure Access Services Edge or just Secure Services Edge can control policy for access to all applications and integrate with your identity system to provision access to all your users with the limited permissions they need. Those agents can also enforce isolation of devices to prevent lateral movement inside your network. And some have remote browser isolation capabilities so that if one of your users visits a malicious website, the malware is detonated in a sandbox in the cloud, not the user's computer."

"What happened to inside-out design?" Dylan asked.

"You did start from the inside. Now you're working your way out to the edge," Aaron answered. "But you're right—there is one thing you're missing. You're using a lot of APIs. Are those another protect surface? Or are they another control?"

"This is another one of your trick questions, isn't it?" Dylan said.

"Is it?" Aaron asked.

"It's both, of course," Dylan said confidently. "We need to remove trust relationships from APIs, don't we?"

"Unfortunately, you're going to need another tool for that. Vic won't like it. But you can make the case. Just like you need a WAF to protect against the OWASP top 10, OWASP has a separate top 10 for API vulnerabilities. It's possible your APIs could be exposed, leaking sensitive info with no audit trail," Aaron said. "Just be sure and let him know that you don't have to have a product.

He can always ask each application administrator to manually review account activity daily. That's a bigger cost in the long run, but at least you're speaking his language at that point."

"So I'm right. It is both," Dylan said.

"Yes," Aaron said reluctantly. "They're a protect surface in that you probably have an API gateway in your service catalog. But with SASE and API security, you'll start to be able to provide more actionable data when it comes to protecting your cloud infrastructure."

"Where do we start?" Dylan asked.

"Same place we always start," Aaron said. "You need an inventory. We need to be able to capture all API traffic with a discovery scan. But we also need to be able to continuously discover new APIs when they're created as well. We need to be able to understand the APIs to be able to detect bad behavior. And the SOC needs to be able to investigate and respond to API threats. You'll need to be able to retain API data for a long time to be able to do historical threat hunting."

"Is that all?" Dylan laughed. "We've got plenty of time for all that before the launch."

"You've made a lot more progress than you think," Aaron said. "Don't forget how far you've come already. But unfortunately, no, that's not all. Zero Trust is about the journey. You'll definitely come up with more trusts you need to remove."

Dylan walked out of the conference room and turned left down the hallway. He turned and pressed the button for the elevator. Dylan was too tired to even hold the phone up to his ear or put it back in his pocket, so he just held it to his side waiting for the elevator.

Boris stepped up beside Dylan, and they both waited for the elevator in silence. Boris was holding his phone reading an email but stopped to look at Dylan. The door to the elevator dinged. Boris got in first, and Dylan walked behind while Boris pressed for the lobby.

"We need to have standards," Dylan said as the doors closed. It was completely silent for several seconds as they stood there.

"You okay, Dylan?" Boris asked.

"I've been thinking about standards," Dylan said.

The doors opened to the lobby. It was dark outside the building. "High standards or low standards?" Boris asked.

"Sky high," Dylan confirmed. "Like cloud standards."

"Oh, you're talking about work," Boris chuckled. "I was worried this was about to get personal or something."

"We talked the other day about Kubernetes."

"Yeah. Security as code. We've already worked in some security testing into our process. We're agile, so we move fast!"

"Did you know that I was hired to be the director of cloud infrastructure?" Dylan asked.

"I hadn't heard. I thought we were going to hire for that position, but I had forgotten about it after the ransomware incident," Boris admitted.

"I almost did too," Dylan said. "We didn't talk about secure container configurations. Those are the standards I was thinking about."

"Sure, we can add some configuration checks," Boris confirmed.

"Can we do a negative check?" Dylan wondered. "Make sure something isn't there?"

"Of course. This is something we already do," Boris said.

"We need to make sure we aren't running the container over a TCP socket. It needs to run as a Unix socket. Can you create a rule to fail the test if it sees a specific command?" Dylan asked.

"Yes. This is easy if you give us the specific command," Boris said.

"I'll get you guys a list. We should also make sure containers aren't being run in privileged mode and not allow any escalations of privilege."

"Oh, cool," Boris said, impressed. "I didn't know there was a command to prevent escalations of privilege. I wish other software had this option."

"We should also create limits on the size of the container and the amount of memory it can use so the containers don't grow out of control," Dylan said. "Also, we should make sure containers can't communicate between each other. And definitely make sure the filesystem is set to read only to prevent any modifications."

"I had no idea this is why you were here," Boris said. "Some of us are going to happy hour down the street. You want to tag along?"

"Yeah. That sounds cool," Dylan said, walking with Boris. "And remind me about container images. We can't just trust that OS images from a third party are secure. We should find a way to automate validation of images," he said as they walked out of the building.

A few hours later, Dylan set his empty pint glass down on the paper napkin. The bar had turned out to be a hole in the wall that he had driven past every day to get to the office. The floors sagged when you walked around. They were missing several balls from the pool table, and there was only one good cue. But he was starting to feel at home. More than that, somehow, he was part of a team.

When he thought about it, things had changed since starting at MarchFit. He didn't run by himself anymore. There was a group that met every morning before work. And he was actually having a drink with some developers, which was weird.

Olivia walked up onto the karaoke stage. She had been drinking in a corner booth and he hadn't noticed she was there.

"LA had been too much for the man," she sang as the opening notes to Glady's Knight's *Midnight Train to Georgia* began playing. Dylan found himself singing along to the backup singers, line along with the rest of the bar.

He thought he had seen everything, but then Rose sat down next to him and waved to the bartender. The bartender set down two shot glasses in front of them and began to pour.

"I'm not sure who to talk to about this," Rose said, pushing his shot glass toward him, then grabbing her own and downing it in one fluid motion.

"Is everything okay?" Dylan asked. He considered for a second, then downed his shot.

"I heard from 3nc0r3 again," Rose admitted.

"Did he post something? I haven't seen any more Twitter notifications," Dylan said, getting out his phone. In all the excitement he hadn't checked his phone a single time.

"No, he contacted me directly," Rose said.

Dylan looked up at her to see if she was serious. "What?" Dylan asked, confused.

"He offered me money to give him information about MarchFit," she said, but as she spoke, she began talking faster. "I didn't tell him anything; I don't understand how he even knows who I am. And he knew things. He knew I was working on Project Zero Trust."

"It's okay. We can check with our SOC to see if they've seen any suspicious activity on your account. We should go on lockdown." He began dialing his phone.

"Sorry, boss, but I don't think that's the play here," Rose said.

"What do you mean?" Dylan asked.

"He's desperate," Rose said. "He wouldn't have targeted me unless he couldn't get in by himself. That means Project Zero Trust is working. He thinks I'm the weak link."

"You shouldn't think that," Dylan started to say.

"Oh, I'm definitely not the weak link," Rose interrupted. "If we ignore him or block him now, he's just going to come back again from some other angle like he's been doing for months. This is our chance to stop him. We're going to reach out to Agent Smecker. "

"You want to set up a sting? Rose, that's amazing. Most people would have probably just kept quiet and taken the money," Dylan said.

"Oh no. I couldn't have spent it. And if I did, I would have gotten caught for tax evasion. And 3nc0r3 would have set me up so I would be looking over my shoulder for years," Rose said. "This is way better."

"Why do you say that?" Dylan asked.

"I'm going to be the one that takes down 3nc0r3," Rose said with a wicked smile. "I'm going to be a legend."

Key Takeaways

In the early days of the Internet, to deploy a new application you had to first build a server, install and harden an operating system, deploy controls like anti-virus, set up the server for logging, and then tailor firewall rules to lock down an application. For some organizations, this process could take weeks or sometimes months, and each step required knowledgeable staff trained on each component of the process.

One of the primary reasons that organizations deploy applications or services to the cloud today is scalability. It can take seconds to deploy a new application in some cases with containers. And cloud service providers have created self-service management portals that allow a single administrator to deploy new services at the push of a button. But this also requires cloud administrators to be familiar not just with one aspect of security, like a firewall, but with all aspects of security to ensure that applications are deployed securely by default. Adding to this complexity is the fact that many organizations must deploy applications not just to one cloud provider but to many different cloud service providers.

Because of this, the "cloud" isn't one protect surface; it's many different protect surfaces.

There are a number of very common issues when it comes to cloud security, like having open cloud storage, not having secure default privileges, not enabling MFA, and not enabling sending logs to the SOC, to name just a few. One of the best ways to help defend all the various cloud protect surfaces is to have robust security requirements built into the project management process itself. This should help address much of the officially sanctioned software at an organization, but it may not capture all shadow IT.

Shadow IT refers to technology systems that aren't managed by the IT department. Because shadow IT services don't follow company policy, this can create potential liabilities for the organization, like not meeting security standards or going through the appropriate contract approval process. Shadow IT isn't limited to cloud services, although the ease with which individuals can create cloud services means they are much more challenging to manage. To provide a more complete picture, regular discovery reports should be run for new services.

One of the challenges with Zero Trust in the cloud is that many applications don't provide the same level of visibility that organizations would have been able to gain if the service were running on premises. Although some cloud applications can be configured to send logs to your SIEM, many applications won't. Some cloud applications may have an API to send this data, but not all. You need insight not just into the application but into specific user activity within the application itself.

A cloud access security broker (CASB) can be deployed in several ways to help provide this visibility. Some organizations choose to operate a CASB as a proxy that can help provide this visibility but may add some latency to applications. CASBs may also require significant customization to provide enough detail into how an application is being used, and when an application is updated it may break the CASB's customization. Alternatively, some vendors provide APIs into their cloud applications. For many common applications like OneDrive, SharePoint, Box, or SalesForce, CASBs have native integrations that allow you to quickly gain visibility to the application.

While the focus of Zero Trust starts from the core of your business and works its way out, you also need to understand the importance of endpoints in your environment. Secure Access Service Edge (SASE) products offer a way of achieving Zero Trust in different environments by allowing an organization to create a software-defined perimeter (SDP). Many organizations have moved to a more flexible model where users work from home, and SDP enables you to ensure that endpoints communicate only with the servers or services that have been approved by policy. In NIST Zero Trust terms, 800-207 creates a conceptual "policy engine," which is integrated with an identity provider and only approved services are allowed. This effectively prevents malware from spreading to SASE-protected endpoints ["via"] lateral movement. SASE-protected endpoints can also be further protected from visiting malicious websites through remote browser isolation so that web pages are run in a sandbox environment, not on the endpoint itself.

One of the biggest blind spots today when it comes to cloud deployments is all of the APIs that interconnect different services. While MarchFit has a WAF and other security controls on the user front end to protect against OWASP top ten attacks like SQL injection or cross-site scripting, there is little visibility on the back end of these web services. The OWASP top ten API vulnerabilities include issues like broken object-level authentication, excessive data exposure, or mass assignment. These vulnerabilities led companies like Peloton, Parler, Facebook, and others to leak vast amounts of data. Even when organizations use encryption to secure their apps, attackers can discover flaws in APIs using man-in-the-middle attacks to reverse-engineer paths and exfiltrate data.

The last phase of the Zero Trust design methodology reminds us to monitor and maintain our cloud protect surfaces. Monitoring API traffic is a great way to gain the same level of visibility into cloud services that many organizations were able to achieve for applications that were on premises. All API calls should be logged for at least a year, similar to how other logs are stored for investigative purposes. An API inventory should be maintained just like other device or data inventories, but because APIs are so dynamic, organizations also need API monitoring tools that can discover APIs in real time and integrate with existing API gateways.

Today, most organizations rely on their SaaS partners to deliver services securely. A cloud service provider is just another third-party vendor, and one of the main protections organizations can use to protect themselves from third parties are contracts. You should have a third-party vendor management program to help address the risks here. Contracts should include specific requirements around notifying you when an incident has occurred (not just breaches). Contract language shouldn't include any limitations of liability for direct damages. Many vendors limit damages to the fees paid for a service, but when personal or other sensitive information is shared with users, the costs to an organization could be significant. Contract provisions should require vendors to have cyber insurance, particularly since two-thirds of all breaches are caused by vendors. Vendors should be required to pay the costs of notifying victims.

Every company is responsible for doing due diligence of vetting the security of their vendors. There are some organizations like Shared Assessments and the Cloud Security Alliance that help provide clarity into the security posture of many vendors. Alternatively, some organizations choose to create their own security questionnaires based on their specific needs. In some cases for extremely large, high-risk vendor contracts, organizations may require evidence of security audits or even conduct their own audits of vendor security. There are also several vendors that provide security ratings services, similar to how Experian and Equifax provide credit ratings for individuals. For all significant technology contracts, IT, security, and legal should review the terms of the agreement and approve them before it is signed. These teams must be able to say "no" to a vendor if their security has significant red flags. And you should be able to get out of a contract if the vendor experiences a breach.

Chapter 9
A Sustainable Culture

Chun Park wasn't a normal celebrity. He was what was known as a walkie-talkie on the MarchFit app. Many of the content creators on the MarchFit network didn't say anything; they just filmed themselves walking or running in lots of different kinds of locations. Often, people at home walking on their desk treadmills were doing other things, like working or talking on the phone, so they just wanted to see some pretty background scenes. The walkie-talkies took a different approach: they would narrate their walks. And these narrated videos were some of the most popular because people would purposefully take a break during the day to go for a walk with someone they enjoyed being with. Chun's voice and calming demeanor were like a mix between Bob Ross and Fred Rogers.

Chun was a retired farmer from Jintai District in China who had taught himself English over the Internet. His children had been successful, and he had moved to the mountains. He joined MarchFit three years ago and took two walks per day through the countryside, once in the morning and once in the afternoon. People thought he was much more like Snow White the way animals would walk right up to him and eat out of his hands.

"Today is a special day, friends," Chun said, beginning his walk on a gravel path, birds singing in the distance. "Security has been very important to me in my life. I know it's important to you, too. MarchFit didn't ask me to say anything, but I've seen how many changes they've made recently. I'm honored to be a part of such a team. If you tap on the information tab, there's some helpful information about protecting your account you should look at."

Inside the MarchFit headquarters, Dylan checked his tie in the bathroom mirror. He was in the washroom outside the executive briefing center (EBC). He had put on his interview suit mostly because it was the only suit that he owned. He came out, and Vic's assistant waved him into the conference room.

The room was full of people that he recognized from TV. They also served on the board of directors for MarchFit. The man sitting next to Vic owned a football team. The woman sitting between Kim and Donna was a technology CEO who was on this month's cover of *Wired*. And he was pretty sure the man at the end of the room sitting by Kofi was a former congressman.

They sat through the financial auditor's presentation. Dylan noticed the former congressman starting to fall asleep, but then it was his turn to speak. As he stood up, his presentation appeared on the video wall behind him without him having to do anything.

"When Noor asked me to brief the board on the status of Project Zero Trust, I was a little nervous." Dylan paused, and several board members laughed. As Dylan looked around the room, everyone was leaning forward, eyes focused on him. "Let's face it, I'm still nervous." That got even more laughs. "I was skeptical at first about Zero Trust. But now that we've been doing it, I can say that we've made one of the best strategic decisions we could have made. That's what Zero Trust is—a strategy for aligning security and the business."

Dylan paused, waiting for any questions. Hearing none, he advanced his PowerPoint slide to the next screen. The only thing on the slide was a number: $6,343,261.

"Zero Trust is about aligning security and the business, that's actually the first step. Over the last several months, I've spent time talking with Donna, our department heads, and other leaders getting to know how our business operates. Partly as a response to our recent breach, we know how much it cost to respond to the malware and get back up and running."

"Isn't six million dollars a little low?" Vic asked. "I thought our total cost was much higher."

"That is correct, Vic," Dylan answered. "It costs us about six million dollars for every hour we're down." There was an audible gasp in the room.

"I thought that our revenue was fixed," one of the board members said. "We lost some monthly subscriptions, but that didn't impact us that much."

"Revenue did take a dip," said Donna. "But all of our costs were still there. We kept our stores open and we continued to pay our content creators even though no one was watching."

"And we know the impact to our brand was also significant," Kofi added. "I assume that's included in this number as well."

Dylan nodded. "From the ransomware incident, we know that it took about thirty-six hours before we were operational," Dylan said.

"You're saying that the real cost of this breach was over two hundred million?" Vic asked.

"Yes," Noor said. "But the real headline here is that this is currently the minimum loss we can expect for any future incident. And we have a high degree of certainty that some kind of cyberattack will happen again."

Dylan advanced to the next slide, which had a list of the different projects that the Zero Trust team had launched over the last several months. There was a timeline labeled "Recovery Timeline" in the center of the screen with thirty-six different hour-long increments. Each Zero Trust project had lines of different thicknesses connected to different segments of the timeline; some were one or two hours, others were six or eight hours wide.

"The focus of Project Zero Trust has been to contain a breach or other incident to the smallest impact possible. After careful analysis of these projects, we've shown how we can reduce the time it will take to recover from an incident from a minimum of thirty-six hours down to eight hours."

The group continued to ask Dylan questions, each bringing up the part of the business most important to them. Dylan stayed after the meeting was over, the executives slowly filing out as he continued to field questions from board members who were curious about different aspects of MarchFit's technology. Looking at his watch, Dylan realized he was late for a debrief with Vic.

Dylan knew the way to Vic's office, but the path was completely different. He was pretty sure new walls had been put up for different meeting areas. There was now a robot security guard patrolling the hallways. It beeped happily as Dylan passed it going into Olivia's old office.

He knocked on the door, then entered. The room had been completely transformed. The carpet had been updated with one large rug dominating one side of the room. The walls had been updated from drywall to a single slab of a stone that Dylan couldn't recognize. There was a wall full of TVs playing different news channels, all on mute. And apparently they had added a real fireplace.

Vic gestured for Dylan to sit at one of the three sofas arranged around three sides of a low coffee table. "You've been putting in new budget requests for new security projects," Vic began. "Even though I told you we needed to focus on the new product launch."

"I've tried to show the business case for each request we've made." Dylan started to respond, but Vic waved him to stop.

"You were right to make those requests, Dylan. I didn't see the big picture when we first talked. But there was a big picture, and those requests helped me see it. Security is one of our core values. Olivia was right to launch Project Zero Trust. I'm starting to see how your strategy is paying off."

"We've made a lot of progress already," Dylan confirmed. "We're on track to complete most of our projects before the product launch in a few weeks."

"That's why I wanted to chat with you. We're going to highlight some of our security enhancements as a part of the launch. We have to acknowledge we've had setbacks. But our competitors are facing similar challenges. We want to set ourselves apart from them based on our commitment to security."

"That's a wonderful idea. I'd love to be able to talk about what we've done on Project Zero Trust. But I'm not sure how much I'm allowed to share," Dylan admitted.

"I love that idea. We can have you work with our product marketing team to have you speak at some conferences. I want you to share the whole story, both the good and the bad. We need to rebuild trust with our clients. What else can we do to show our commitment?"

"We were actually just talking about cloud security. The Cloud Security Alliance has a registry of companies that have gone through a certification process to show they have the right security controls for the cloud. We could start working on that, but I don't think it will be ready in time for the launch."

"I don't know if it has felt that way for the last couple of months, Dylan, but you've got my full support. Some people say you need support at the top to make security happen. Others say it's better to have grassroots support. You've got both here. I'm actually a little excited to see what happens at your tabletop exercise," Vic said, standing up and extending his hand to Dylan. "You ready?"

"We're getting there." Dylan stood up and shook Vic's hand.

It took several minutes to walk downstairs, but Dylan was pretty sure that Zero Trust Central, or ZTC as Harmony referred to the basement conference room, didn't have disco lights the last time he was there. And there was some strange electronic big band music playing softly in the background. But the whole team was back together for the first time in what felt like weeks. Rose walked up to Dylan and offered a red Solo cup. He wasn't sure what was in it, so he gave it a sniff before taking a sip. "It's too bad we never applied the Zero Trust principles to our security awareness training," Dylan said, thinking about the upcoming tabletop exercise.

"What are you talking about?" Rose said. "Of course I applied the Zero Trust methodology to security awareness. The protect surface is people. The transaction flow is the life cycle of the employee from the interview process to the day they leave the company or retire. Sorry, I thought this was obvious."

"No, go on!" Dylan exclaimed.

"Like we talked about in the beginning, it's more effective to secure something at the beginning, so we start with new hire orientation. But then we're rebuilding all of our IT or HR training to intentionally include elements of cybersecurity, from learning Excel to how to be a good manager. Creating policy is all about customizing the user's experience, so we offer several different tracks for security-specific training as well, based on different roles in the organization. Do you want to see our training plan?"

"Uh, heck yes. That sounds amazing," Dylan said, thinking about the implications. "But we should start the meeting." The rest of the room had gone quiet listening to them talk. Harmony had joined the Zoom call and the SOC team manager, Luis, and Chris were both on the call. Peter Liu and Noor joined a few seconds later as Harmony admitted people into the meeting from the waiting room.

"Let's get started. We've only got a week left before the tabletop exercise. We'll review the scenario at the end, but I wanted to start with logistics first." Dylan paused for a moment, waiting for any questions. "I wanted to start with the invitation list. I'd love to invite everyone in the company, but our biggest conference room is only big enough for about sixty people, and that's standing room only."

"Why don't we do the meeting virtually?" Brent asked.

"We find that when the people participating are all in the same room, the conversation is much more dynamic," Chris said. "There are fewer distractions from other work and it simulates a bit of the tension from the real thing."

"Particularly since that conference room is also the same place we had our first briefing about the ransomware campaign almost six months ago," Noor added.

"Let's record the tabletop, but most people probably won't want to watch the whole thing," Rose said. "We can edit it down and make the most important parts into a training video."

"I think that's a great idea," Dylan said. "We'll have a Zoom option, but that group will just be for observers. Vic wants to be there in person. We should invite Olivia, Kofi, Donna, and Kim at a minimum for the in-person event. Who else should we invite?"

"Agent Smecker should be there, if he's not busy with something else," Rose said, smiling slightly.

"Our moderator will facilitate the tabletop," Chris said. "He'll be coordinating with Peter, your security consultant, to perform the actual penetration testing. Luis will be monitoring the SOC and will raise an alarm if the SOC sees anything."

"What happens if they don't see anything?" Peter asked.

"We'll keep going with the scenario, following the prompts, and see how far you can get. We'll take down all our notes and use those as next steps for improving our visibility and controls," Dylan said.

"One point of warning," Chris said. "We want to be able to simulate a real-world scenario. Sometimes things happen in the real world that can impact your incident response. So you should also be prepared for some key personnel to have unexpected family emergencies and have to step away. Everyone should have a backup that's ready to step in."

Rose was standing in front of a large video camera perched on a tall tripod. There was a fuzzy microphone hanging above her and a green screen just behind her. The room she was in had been designed as a training lab with rows of computers where people would go for training. Since most of the workforce at March-Fit was still working remotely, they had removed the first three rows of desks and created a virtual studio. There were still several rows of desks at the back of the room that had been spread out for socially distanced in-person training.

Fiona, the production manager, came into the room, peering through the camera lens to check the image. There were a number of people already in the Zoom session. She gave a thumbs-up to Rose and said, "Whenever you're ready." She pressed the record button in Zoom and stepped back to watch Rose.

"Collaboration is the most important thing we do here at MarchFit," Rose said. "And it's more important than ever that we work together securely. We've got a number of different collaboration tools we support, from Slack to Microsoft Teams, but your departments may also use their own specialized collaboration tools."

The screen displaying the chat window started to scroll with different people commenting about the tools they use in their departments, from software issue tracking to project management software.

"One of the best ways to remind us to be secure is to think about the people we're protecting." Rose displayed a MarchFit promotional video on mute so she could continue talking. "It's easy to forget we're protecting real people. We encourage you to take some of the pictures of our users and print them to remind ourselves who we are protecting." Several clapping icons appeared over the pictures of the people on the call and several more wrote encouraging messages in the chat window.

"We have some security controls that we put around all our tools, like Single Sign On, or SSO, or multifactor authentication. So if your app doesn't have that enabled, let us know. These help us protect the applications, but they also give us auditing in case something does happen. Today, we'll be focusing on how to get the most out of Slack and Teams specifically, but before we dive in on how to use them, there are several security best practices that we should all be aware of for any application we use."

Fiona cleared her throat, "One of the comments in chat asked if it's okay to use text messages as your MFA?"

"Great question," Rose said. "The short answer is that SMS messages for MFA aren't as secure as other options. The long answer is that the bad guys do this thing called SIM-jacking. They can call your phone company pretending to be you and say that they've just bought a new phone. They have your account transferred to the SIM card that they put in a burner phone. So then, all the MFA messages you were getting via text to your phone go straight to the bad guy."

The chat window started to scroll faster than Rose could read the comments.

"There are two other things that you should know in general before we dive in further. First, we should never trust that our tools are completely secure. And second, we should plan for things to go wrong. You guys probably know this already, but we never share passwords on Slack or Teams. Because we don't trust these systems, we don't want to put sensitive info out there that could be exposed. We have other secure systems for sharing sensitive data."

"What about contractors?" Fiona asked

"I'm glad you asked," Rose said. "Sometimes we will need to give our contractors access to some of our collaboration tools. This is a necessary part of the business. But we don't have to set those accounts up to last forever. For guest access, we should always set the accounts to expire after a short period of time, like a week or a month. We can always renew the account if we need to. But we've seen from experience that if we set a guest account up to last forever, we'll invariably forget to shut it down once the contractor leaves. And this is a great way for the bad guys to get in."

In the ZTC, Dylan, Harmony, Brent, and Nigel were listening in to an intel briefing from an analyst working for their industry Information Security Advisory Council (ISAC). Harmony pressed the mute button on her laptop. "I can't believe that we didn't join this ISAC years ago. This is some of the best information we've gotten," she said.

"I thought it was going to cost a lot more to become a member," Dylan admitted. "But it's just a few thousand dollars per year. We've only been a part of the ISAC for a few days now, but just seeing all of the emails in the discussion list makes me think this was the best investment we've made in a while."

"Did you see that one with the IP addresses of some Russian threat actors who were targeting several large retail organizations?" Nigel asked.

"Yes. I've blocked them at our firewalls," Harmony said. "But we can start incorporating some of their threat feeds to do that automatically. But I bet there's a way to validate those feeds instead of trusting them blindly. I'll have to look into that."

"I'll have to tell Boris about the threat actors who are targeting organizations that use our underlying tech stack," Nigel said. "Now that we know more about what they're targeting, we can do something about it."

"Careful with how we share info," Dylan reminded him. "We've got to follow their classification system for sharing, even inside MarchFit," he said, looking at Brent.

"Why is everyone looking at me?" Brent said, chuckling.

Isabelle was standing next to Rose in front of the green screen. Fiona shared the screen on her laptop, showing a slide deck that read "Project Management 101." The training was developed for managers, but Isabelle hoped to make this a recurring training through HR. The head of HR, Mia Wallace, and several of her staff were in the room at one of the back tables, watching in person.

"Okay, before we get started with the training, we're going to do something new," Isabelle said. "It's called the security minute. We're going to talk about a security issue for the first sixty seconds of each meeting we have from now on. We encourage you to do this in your team gatherings or project briefings, whatever feels most appropriate. Don't worry—we'll email you all several topics you can bring up each week."

The group of HR staff at the back of the room began taking notes.

"The security minute for this week is about passwords," Rose continued. "By a show of hands, how many of you reuse your passwords on multiple sites?" Nearly half of the people in the Zoom raised their hands. All of the HR staff raised their hands. "I'm going to tell you all a secret," Rose said, "I don't actually know any of my passwords. We recommend using a password vault. This can store your passwords across multiple devices. But the best part is that it can create a random super long password that's unique for every site you visit. And we want to encourage people to have sites remember your password. This can be a great way of helping you recognize when you've clicked on a phishing site that is trying to steal your password, because it won't already be remembered by your device. Remember, if you don't know your password, you can't give it away."

"Isn't this just like how airline attendants go over the safety information at the beginning of each flight?" Isabelle asked like they had rehearsed.

"Yes, it's exactly like that," Rose confirmed. "We're giving out information that may or may not be new to people. But the real message we're sending with the security minute is that in the culture of our organization, we want our teams to know that we value security. We value it so much that it's the first thing we talk about. And our goal will be that it's the first thing that everyone in our organization does."

"Now let's talk about my favorite subject—projects," Isabelle said. "Security should also be the first thing we think about in our projects. For some larger projects, we'll have someone from IT designated to be the security liaison for a project. Smaller projects should designate someone for this role, like a deputy."

"For this training," Rose continued, "we're going to have a case study as the project we'll be managing. We're going to plan for a hypothetical MarchFit developer conference."

"That might actually happen someday," Isabelle confirmed.

"And we'll be extra prepared by having done this already," Rose said. "But the first thing we're going to do is what we call a premortem. Most people wait till the end of a project to think about what went wrong. We're going to flip that and talk about what might go wrong. Then we'll talk about what we're going to do about it. And then plan for it."

Dylan walked into the training studio. Mia and some of her staff were talking quietly at their table, so Dylan sat down at one of the other tables. Isabelle and Rose thanked the audience for attending their class, then came over to talk with Dylan about the tabletop exercise.

As Dylan was about to start talking, Mia walked up to the table.

"Great class," Mia said. "This is one of the best ones you've put together. And I love how you're working security into your training."

"Thank you!" Rose and Isabelle said at the same time.

"I've been thinking about our security awareness training," Mia said.

"I know. We're building a whole new awareness program," Rose said.

"Have you thought about how you measure how much people are changing? How their habits are changing over time?" Mia asked.

"We have some quizzes that we're building," Rose said. "And we're measuring engagement."

"I'm wondering if you might be interested in incorporating your security training into our wellness program?" Mia asked. "We know that fifty percent of all human behavior is based on habits. Our wellness program is about changing behaviors. It seems to me that our security training should be focused on changing bad habits in exactly the same way."

"That makes sense," Dylan said.

"And as a part of the wellness program, there's already a core group of people who participate in every activity," Mia said. "If we can change our employee security habits, that could have a big impact. And we can measure behavior change for security just like we measure other behavior changes with our wellness program."

Brent and Nigel were standing in front of the EBC's espresso machine while it automatically ground the beans before making a perfect cappuccino. Brent picked it up and breathed in the aroma. Sighing, he added a single spoonful of sugar to the cup and began stirring slowly. Nigel picked up his own cup and turned to see a young IT guy in a green polo shirt standing at the door of the EBC looking in. When Nigel made eye contact, the guy knocked on the door to the EBC, then waved to the two of them. Brent shrugged and walked over to open the door, holding his coffee gingerly in his other hand.

"I think that's Simon, the new guy from the help desk," Nigel said, peering into the grinder as he brewed his own cup. Brent opened the door without saying anything.

"Are you guys supposed to be in here?" Simon asked.

"Our cards let us in," Brent answered.

The guy looked around, "Can I get a cup of coffee too?"

"Does your card work?" Nigel asked. Simon swiped his card, and it beeped at him in annoyance and flashed red, indicating that he did not, in fact, have access.

"Come on, guys. I'm dying for some caffeine," Simon begged.

"Just one cup," Nigel said protectively. "But we're not letting you tailgate around with us into the data center because we're coffee chums."

Brent shrugged, and Simon walked into the room over to where Nigel was standing. Nigel stepped out of the way so Simon could make his own cup. Simon stood there for a moment while thinking about all his choices and then pressed the button for an Americano. He had forgotten to put the mug underneath, and the coffee started dripping before he realized. He started making the coffee over again.

"I can't believe it, but I just had to help a person change their password. They couldn't figure out the portal, so I walked over in person."

Nigel and Brent stood side by side drinking their coffees. "Why'd they need to change their password?" Brent asked.

"Oh, they clicked on a phishing link. They realized they had done it, and called to let us know. But you know what they say: People are the weakest link."

"Uh-oh," Nigel said.

"What?" Simon asked.

"We don't say that around Brent," Nigel said.

"People aren't the weakest link," Brent corrected. "People are the only link."

"But I thought we are doing Zero Trust? We shouldn't trust anyone, right?"

"That's not what Zero Trust is," Brent said. "I thought the same way you do. But Zero Trust requires us to work as a team. We can't be a team without trusting each other. Zero Trust isn't about individuals; it's about packets. We have to trust each other to do our jobs, but we don't have to trust the packets that are attached to that individual through the devices and networks that are the lifeblood of our organization."

"I didn't realize that. I just heard that almost all breaches are caused by people or human error," Simon said.

"Believing something is true makes it true," Nigel said. "It happens so often, there's actually a name for it. It's called the Pygmalion effect. Our beliefs about people influence our actions; our actions impact what other people believe about themselves; and their actions reinforce our beliefs. The most important part of being successful at something is believing that it's possible." Nigel sipped his coffee thoughtfully.

Simon just blinked for several seconds. He had not been expecting a philosophical discussion. He picked up his Americano and took a drink while he thought about that.

"Zero Trust isn't about being cynical," Brent explained. "Cynicism is a shortcut so you don't have to think critically about anything because it's all bad. Zero Trust is about finding where trust relationships are inside a system and surgically removing trust without breaking the system. That takes a lot of understanding of how the business works. That takes a deep understanding of technology. And we have to apply our knowledge while trusting the team we're working for," Brent said. "We've all worked with security guys who liked to bang their hands on their desk and explain why we can't do things. We've got to be better than that. Zero Trust helps us say yes. When we know we can remove trust from services, we can do things we wouldn't have been able to do before. If we say no, people just go someplace else to solve their problem, and that creates shadow IT, and we can't help secure something we don't know about. Because we help people do things instead of saying no, all the shadow IT out there is coming back in, and we're making it secure too."

Dylan sat down at the conference room table late to the meeting. He had gotten used to working remotely, and travel time between meetings was one of the biggest annoyances of coming back to the office. Noor was speaking, but Dylan looked around the room at some of the IT staff that he hadn't had a chance to work with. They all had their laptops out and some were clicking or tapping on their keyboards. Another annoyance for in-person meetings that he had forgotten about. Dylan looked at the stickers on the different engineers' laptops. Among the various technology or science fiction stickers, he kept seeing different versions of stickers with the number zero on them.

Dylan realized each sticker corresponded to one of the protect surfaces that the Project Zero Trust team had defined several months ago. Some of the engineers had multiple stickers. Dylan realized they were publicly displaying all the protect surfaces that they were responsible for protecting.

He also noticed that Harmony had the most stickers out of everyone in the room. He'd have to ask her where she was getting them.

He private messaged her on his laptop. It turned out that each team created their own sticker after prodding by Harmony. One of the guys was married to a graphic designer and had created theirs to look like WWII bomber nose art. Some had flames or shields. Some were text based and read "PZT DNS Squadron." The identity team had a superhero with a lowercase "i" on his chest with a zero for the dot over it. It seemed like their team had grown from just the six of them to the whole company before he realized it.

Several minutes later, Dylan was waiting at the elevator to go downstairs. It had been a long day, and he closed his eyes for a moment and imagined taking a nap. His reverie was short lived as he heard the click of a pair of heels next to him and smelled lilacs. He opened his eyes to see Isabelle standing next to him. They rode the elevator downstairs in silence. They left the elevator and began to walk toward the exit.

"I've been meaning to thank you, Dylan," she said, stopping just before the door.

"Thank me?" Dylan asked as he stopped to face her. "Did I do something right for a change?" he asked jokingly.

"Oh, no," she explained. "It's not any one thing. It's more like what you didn't do. I got my start as a project manager in manufacturing. I knew Olivia from those days and she brought me on to help build out our capacity for making our own treadmills. After that, I stayed around and became the head of the project management office."

"Oh, I had no idea," Dylan admitted. "That's really interesting, but I'm still not sure why you're thanking me." Several people came and went past them, so they both moved a little more out of the way of the flow of traffic.

"All our IT project managers were tied up when we started Project Zero Trust. That meant I was the only one not working on the recovery efforts, which is why I began working with you."

"Sounds just like how I got pulled into Zero Trust," Dylan said.

"I didn't know the first thing about IT, so it was a pretty steep learning curve for me. Anyway, I wanted to thank you because you never made me feel bad for not knowing some of the acronyms or jargon you guys were using," she said. "That really made me feel like I was part of the team."

"You're welcome," Dylan said. "You were a really important part of the team! We couldn't have accomplished so much without you," Dylan said. They opened the door to the sun setting over the horizon as they walked to their cars.

Several hours later, Rose was with Agent Smecker, sitting at the table in a hotel room, with men in suits walking past them in hurried steps. There was a knock at the door and everyone froze in place. They all turned toward the door in unison. "Pizza," said a voice from outside the room. The nearest agent propped open the door and the delivery kid took a step back when he saw all the people in the room.

"You're not going to make me wear a wire, are you?" Rose asked jokingly after the kid had gone.

"Of course we are," Agent Smecker answered, handing her what looked like a pen but actually concealed a microphone in the tip. She slid it inside the pocket of the blazer she was wearing and tapped the mic a couple times. The tech across from them gave her a thumbs-up, then went back to typing.

Rose looked at the bank of laptops spread across the large welcoming table where the flower arrangement would have been in the lobby of the suite. The flowers had been placed on the floor. In their place there were twenty-four different camera views of the coffee shop across from the street where Rose would meet 3nc0r3. She recognized the tall agent wearing a black leather jacket who had just left the room sitting by the front window of the café.

"Do you want to go over the script again?" Smecker asked.

"Get him to confirm transfer of the money," she said. "Make him admit as much as possible. But don't sound like I'm getting him to admit anything. I'll start small, like I was wondering if this little glitch I saw was really him. And then I'll build up his ego by talking about how everyone at the office treats him like the bogeyman whenever something goes wrong. I'll try and sound disgruntled while I'm doing it."

"That's him," the tech said as a young man rounded the corner and went inside the shop. Almost everyone in the room stood up right at that exact moment.

"All right, time to go," Rose said, smiling, and grabbed her purse to leave.

Key Takeaways

Success with Zero Trust starts with creating a supportive culture.

A culture of security starts at the top. But trust with business leaders is earned. Security teams shouldn't simply ask for an unlimited budget and expect to get everything they ask for. Over the last several chapters, there were also numerous cases where the team used existing tools to solve their challenges without new budget requests. The team also wrote multiple business justifications for the different projects that were necessary to achieve MarchFit's goals. This is where a strategy of Zero Trust can help. Zero Trust helps define the big picture, and each business case should be aligned with this overall strategy. This helps connect the dots for leadership on how to achieve the overall goal of containing cyber incidents.

When it comes to security awareness training, people are the protect surface. All employees have a life cycle, from when they are interviewing to when they leave the organization or retire. Your culture is defined by the expectations, processes, behaviors, and rituals that your organization puts into practice every day. These can all be influenced by training and reinforced by policies. But security awareness should also be progressive so that employees continue to learn and grow as they progress in their careers. Training messages should be tailored and customized based on specific roles inside the organization as well.

There are many different ways today to help teams collaborate. Tools like SharePoint, Slack, and other apps enable teams that are spread out all over the world to share and innovate much more quickly than in the past. These tools also require us to continually adapt the way we as individuals apply security to all these new and different types of tools. Sometimes this means we have to change our behaviors to better fit our circumstances.

Fifty percent of all human behaviors are based on habits. To have a chance at improving our security outcomes, we need to make critical security behaviors into a habit. To measure behavior change, we should also examine our cybersecurity habits. Creating habits as a group using techniques like the security minute can help teams embrace a strong culture of cybersecurity.

Cybersecurity is often scary for individuals. It's technically challenging, and there are very real consequences for not getting it right. We need to help everyone on our teams build an identity so that they believe they are capable of playing a role in security. Zero Trust requires us to be proactive in order to prevent bad things from happening. This can involve work, so following Zero Trust principles can feel easy when we make that work into a habit.

We don't need to get everyone involved on day one to be successful. Research from David Centola and his colleagues at the University of Pennsylvania indicates that to create long-term sustainable change, we only need twenty-five percent of a group to adopt new behaviors for the group as a whole to change their collective behaviors (https://penntoday.upenn.edu/news/damon-centola-tipping-point-large-scale-social-change). And by partnering with HR and their wellness program, a big percentage of this goal is already within reach of many organizations.

It is essential to create a culture that embraces Zero Trust. This means broadening the conversation. When we talk about cybersecurity (and Zero Trust specifically), we bring everyone in: all of IT, finance, human resources, legal, risk, and even the board. The first question our business leaders ask about Zero Trust is:

"What do you mean, we can't trust?" To be successful in running an organization, we need trust. Trust is the currency of business.

We trust people, not packets.

There's also a trap to Zero Trust. One of the most common mistakes that people make when they are on their Zero Trust journey is that we shouldn't trust people. Trusting people is the most critical thing that we can do to enable success on a Zero Trust journey. Zero Trust focuses on removing trust relationships from digital systems because trust is what threat actors exploit to obtain unauthorized access.

Trust is also what makes all human relationships possible and it's what makes businesses operate.

In security, and particularly with Zero Trust, it's easy to fall into the trap of cynicism. If we don't trust anything, then we don't have to apply any effort to analyzing situations. But when working with others we need to build trust in order to accomplish our goals. Project Zero Trust requires building a coalition of many different groups within an organization, from IT to HR, legal, finance, risk, and audit.

In his book *Speed of Trust* (Simon and Schuster, 2006), Stephen Covey argues that we need to have high trust at the same time that we apply analysis in order to have good judgment. If we never trust but only have skepticism of those around us, we're left with indecision and we can make no progress. The absence of trust can actually be a tax on organizations that slows progress and keeps individuals and organizations from reaching their full potential. When security teams are cynical, the organization suffers.

Our secret motto in security is "people are the weakest link." If we believe this, we're setting ourselves up for failure—first, because the statement is wrong and, second, because of the way it changes the way we act. People are the largest attack surface in our organizations. It's more accurate to say that people are the only link in the chain when it comes to security.

In the 1960s, Harvard psychologist Robert Rosenthal described an effect where expectations led subjects in an experiment to turn those expectations into reality. He partnered with an elementary school principal, Lenore Jacobson, and together they told teachers at the school that the worst-performing students were actually the best and that the best performers were the worst (Rosenthal & Jacobson (1968), Pygmalion in the Classroom, *Urban Review* 3(1): 16–20). At the end of the year, they tested the students again, and the students who the teachers believed were the best (but had actually been the worst) had outperformed their classmates. If we persist in believing that people are the weakest link, then we will make that belief into reality.

Chapter 10
The Tabletop Exercise

ylan, Brent, and Harmony were in the ZTC basement conference room standing in front of the projection screen. The lights in the room were actually working for the first time. The conference table in the center of the room had been replaced with two large desks in an L shape. Shelves of old equipment lined the walls behind the desks. A green couch and three pieces of furniture formed a U shape. An old rug had been placed in the middle of the U shape, with the projection screen at the open end. The desks were covered with stickers. And Dylan noticed a red door on the other side of the room for the first time.

"What's behind that red door?" Dylan asked.

Harmony almost spit out the drink she was taking. "Oh, nothing. It's just a boring old storeroom where we keep our snibbets."

"What's a snibbet?" Dylan asked.

"It's a kind of plange," Harmony explained.

"Are you making an *IT Crowd* reference?" Dylan laughed as he recalled the dialogue from the BBC TV comedy from the 2000s. Brent hadn't gotten the reference.

"Maybe," Harmony said with just the faintest hint of a smile. "Oh, look, Chris and Peter are joining the call." Their Zoom video feed popped up and the three of them turned to the screen and began talking.

"I've done a tabletop exercise before, and it seems like a good idea to do one, but is that really a Zero Trust project?" Brent asked the group without looking up from his laptop.

"Part of the monitor and maintain phase means that we need to be regularly evaluating whether our controls are good enough or whether we have any blind spots," Dylan answered. "A tabletop exercise is a great way of doing that."

"Isn't this just a clever way of playing Dungeons and Dragons at work?" Harmony asked.

Brent stopped typing the email he was working on and closed his laptop. "Right. Just talking through a scenario might be fun, but will that really change anything?" Brent asked.

"There are several different kinds of tabletop exercise," Chris explained. "The most basic is pretty similar to a Dungeons and Dragons campaign. You've got a moderator that functions just like a Dungeon Master. The moderator will have developed a guide for how the scenario will evolve."

"You sound like you've got some experience as a DM," Harmony observed.

"But we're not just doing a regular campaign. I mean tabletop," Chris said. "What we're planning is more like a live-fire training exercise. Some people might call it a purple teaming exercise."

"What's a purple team?" Brent asked.

"In cybersecurity circles, a red team is a group that tries to break into things. A blue team is the group that plays defense. Sometimes we will do exercises that simulate a real-world event, and the red and blue teams don't communicate. A purple team is more of a collaborative approach to a simulation where both sides work together."

"So, that means the penetration tester and the SOC will be on the call with us and will respond just like they would in real life?" Brent asked.

"Yes, they'll be monitoring in real time. They might actually alert on a real alert or two since they won't know what Peter is doing versus what is real. But we'll also script much of the work that the penetration tester will perform in advance to create the most realistic scenario. He'll be doing some scanning in advance to make sure there are real findings."

"With all the work with Zero Trust, won't this tabletop scenario be pretty simple? We won't really be able to find anything, right?" Brent asked.

"Trust me—there are always more trusts that you can remove." Chris laughed for a second, but then he became serious. "I don't know this for sure, but I get the impression that some people think of a penetration test as a kind of CYA. They hope that the tests will show that they don't have any issues or to show off how good the security team is. One of the reasons that I started my company was that

I didn't feel like I was getting our money's worth doing a penetration test unless we found something to help make us better. The goal is to always be getting better."

"Every step matters," Dylan said.

"Every step matters," Chris agreed.

"So how do we build this Dungeon Master guide?" Harmony asked.

Chris laughed. "In tabletop exercises, we call it an MSEL, or Master Scenario Events List. The MSEL comes from the NIST standard for developing and running tabletop exercises. It's NIST 800-84 if you want to look it up. But first we need to start with defining our objectives. Those might change based on the audience, but in our case I think we should go with a mix of technical and procedural objectives."

"One of the most important things that I've heard from Vic and Noor from the last incident is that we can't have another incident shut us down," Dylan said. "If we were to lose that much revenue again, it might mean going out of business."

"That's a perfect objective for a live-fire exercise," Chris said. "The penetration tester will stop before they do anything that could impact operations, of course. The way that I would write that as an objective for the MSEL would be 'Can the team keep the organization operational during an incident?'"

"Definitely," Peter said.

"One of the things that I was concerned about are false positives," Harmony said. "We're always getting notifications from the SOC that sound really scary. Sometimes we have to drop everything to investigate, and it turns out to be a server we didn't know about talking to a new service no one ever heard of. But both are legit."

"That's definitely something we love testing in a tabletop," Chris said. "We always want to include red herrings into the scenario to simulate the confusion that can happen in a real incident. We will include some red herrings into the scenario, but for the MSEL, we'll ask whether the team can tell the difference between a real issue and a false positive."

"I've been working with our business partners in our different departments and I'm a little concerned that they don't know our procedures well enough," Brent said. "How do we test that?"

"That will definitely come out during the assessment," Chris said. "We don't just want the IT guys to answer questions. We'll be asking different department heads what they would do in different situations. The objective here will be to identify specific gaps, not just in technology controls but also incident response procedures, resources, or training that could impact the organization if this were a real incident."

"Holy cow," Harmony said. "This is really happening!"

Several days later, Dylan felt a little like James Bond dressed in a new black suit. He looked at his watch. Again. Everyone on the Project Zero Trust team was gathered at the bottom of the stairs except for Brent. He had sent a message to the group to all meet at the briefing center early, then walk in as a team. Rose was wearing a vintage black and white dress with a new pair of glasses. Harmony had ditched her usual hoodie for a pair of black slacks and a white shirt and white blazer. Isabelle was in a black suit and crisp white shirt, jacket draped over her shoulder. Even Nigel had donned a white shirt in place of his usual red arsenal jersey.

Noor walked up behind Dylan. "You all wore matching outfits?" she asked.

"We were hoping to coordinate with you," Rose said. Noor was wearing her traditional black pantsuit, a white shirt, and her trademark black tie.

"Well, now I guess we can all walk in like that scene from *Reservoir Dogs*," Noor said. Without waiting to see the stunned looks on their faces, Noor began walking up the stairs. Rose, Harmony, Nigel, and Isabelle took their places alongside Noor. Dylan didn't want to be late, so he followed the group up the stairs, giving one last look to see if Brent was coming.

Brent was already in the briefing center, also wearing a black suit. He was making cappuccinos for the attendees as they trickled in. "Where were you guys?" Brent asked. "I thought we were all meeting here early?"

"We were waiting for you downstairs!" Harmony laughed.

Most of the attendees had already arrived. The executive briefing center tables had been configured in a U shape, with Chris standing at the open end of the U. Each place setting at the table had a binder with a label that read "Situation Manual" and a glass of water. Vic was leaning over discussing something with Kofi and Kim. Boris was laughing loudly at something Agent Smecker had just said. Peter and Luis were both remote, their faces displayed on the video wall along with several members of the IT staff that were watching remotely so they didn't have too many people in the conference room.

Chris cleared his throat and began the meeting. "Good morning! For those of you who don't know me, I'm Chris Grey. I'm the founder of one of your security services partners and I'll be your moderator for this exercise. We've carefully built this scenario in partnership with Dylan and the Project Zero Trust team over the last several months. It was a little challenging coming up with a new scenario for a tabletop exercise, given how much MarchFit has been through over the last six months. What you have in front of you is the situation manual that will provide the background on this exercise and will set the stage for the events that are about to take place. But first, I'd like to ask for a round of applause for all the work that the Project Zero Trust team has put into this exercise and the effort that has gone into making MarchFit's security that much better."

Everyone in the room began clapping. Vic stood up, and the rest of the room followed suit. Brent leaned over and patted Dylan on the back.

Chris continued. "For this tabletop, we'll be running on scenario time. We'll be going a little faster than real life so that we can focus on specific stages of the incident. The response could take days or weeks, so keep that in mind. Luis is on the line. He's with our SOC. Say hello, Luis."

"Hello, Luis," Luis said. The group chuckled at this.

"Peter Liu is MarchFit's penetration tester, and he'll be playing the role of a cybercriminal. Peter will be performing some scripted testing that we've agreed to in advance. If Luis is able to detect Peter's activity, he'll chime in and let us know. Any questions before we start?" Chris paused and looked around the room. "Hearing none. It's 8:35 a.m.," Chris began. "The manager of the customer support hotline emails Noor that several customers report that their TreadMarch units appear to start but are only displaying a blue screen and will not connect to the network. What do you do?"

Everyone in the room turned to Noor. "It's probably too soon to panic," she said, which got a huge laugh from the room. "I'd ask the manager for more information about the devices. Is there a common denominator like the locations, firmware, or age of the devices? I'd also want to look at our change control to see if we had made any recent changes."

"Is there someone we can dispatch to physically go out to see one of the treadmills?" Vic asked.

"Yes, we can dispatch a local third-party technician. They are probably already working on other support tickets, so we'd need to pull them off a job and reroute."

"How long would it take to dispatch a technician?" Chris asked.

"Probably thirty minutes, best case," Noor answered. "Maybe forty-five with traffic."

"Noted," Chris said. "The technician will provide a report at 9:30. What other information will you need?" He typed several notes into the MSEL guide for the debrief after the tabletop.

"Boris, have you ever seen an error like this before?" Dylan asked.

Boris was seated at the end of the U, nearest to Chris. "No," Boris answered, turning to talk to the group. "We don't have an error page that displays a blue screen that I know of."

"Don't we have a monitoring center where we can see the status of all our treadmills?" Vic asked.

"We don't have a real-time view," Boris said, scratching his head. "We run daily reports on activity and usage, but we've never put together a dashboard where we could do this live. We could probably pull something together in about a week."

"It's now 8:45," Luis interrupted. "Hi, Harmony. I'm from the SOC and one of our team members has detected suspicious activity on several user accounts."

"What do you mean by suspicious?" Harmony asked.

"Our behavioral-based detections indicate that the activities were out of the ordinary for those users," Luis explained into the camera, his face lit by his computer monitors. "We can provide you the ID numbers of those users, but I don't have any further information at this time."

"Okay, I'll start looking at the activity for those users," Harmony said.

Noor was about to speak, but Chris interrupted. "At this point, I should point out that Noor and customer support are aware of the issues with the treadmills, but the team hasn't sent any further communications inside the organization about the issue. So, Harmony, you're not aware that the treadmills are having issues."

"When do we send notices that something is going wrong?" Vic asked, looking around the room.

"We're almost always troubleshooting an issue," Noor said, adjusting her tie so that it was straight. "The challenge is knowing when something is systemic. For a single device, that's low priority and our help desk will resolve it. Our incident response plan says that if we reach a threshold of 1 percent of our devices, we raise the issue to a medium-level category, and we'll respond by forming the incident response team. If it's more than 10 percent of devices, that's a high-level event. In practice, all events start out as a low-level notice, and as we investigate the event will go up in priority."

"It's now 9 a.m.," Chris said, looking down at his computer for the next injection prompt. "Noor gets another report from the call center. It's nothing urgent, but they're letting her know that the call volume seems higher than normal for a weekday and are asking if it's okay to increase staffing to meet the demand."

"How much higher is the call volume?" Kim asked, leaning forward.

"It's about fifteen percent higher," Chris replied.

"Does that make this a high-level incident?" Vic asked.

"This is the Tuesday before Thanksgiving," Noor said. "It could be that more people are off work and are around to call for support during the day. But in practice, when something like this happens, I will usually send an email to the IT leadership team giving them a heads-up just in case."

"It's now 9:30 scenario time," Chris said. "The technician dispatched to look at one of the malfunctioning treadmills has gotten it functional again. He had to reinstall the firmware, but the device is back online. He did note that one of his repairmen reported that the security dongle they use to securely access the treadmills had gotten lost several days ago."

"Why are we only just now learning about this?" Kim asked, crossing her arms and leaning back in her chair.

"The technician indicates the repairman thought it was only misplaced, and they had been looking for it during their day off. So this was the first day that the technician knew about it."

"What could someone do with a security dongle?" Kim asked.

"It can give them full access to a treadmill," Boris answered. "But they can only use it on one treadmill at a time."

"Is there a way to duplicate the device? Or make it work virtually so they could manipulate multiple treadmills?" Kim asked.

"It's possible. We'd have to look into that," Boris answered.

"It's now 10:07," Chris said. "After reviewing the logs, Harmony called one of the users that she happened to know personally. It turns out that the employee is currently on vacation and does not have access to a computer."

"I think we can definitely bump this up to a medium-level incident now," Noor said, adjusting the papers in her stack.

Chris cleared his throat. "It's now 10:15. April, your PR department reports that there have been several tweets complaining about working conditions in one of MarchFit's factories overseas. After several reshares of the tweets, people have begun commenting that they are planning a protest outside the MarchFit headquarters later today."

"How many protesters are we expecting?" Kim asked.

"Unknown at this time," Chris said.

"I'll put in a call to our security contractor," Kim said, pretending to pick up her cell phone to make a call. "We may want to bring in some extra personnel in case there's a large group."

"It's now 10:29," Chris said. "I'm sorry to report that Noor has gotten a call from her child's school. Her child is sick and since her spouse is out of town, she needs to leave to take her sick child to the doctor. Noor will no longer be available for the scenario."

"I had expected something like this might happen," Noor said smiling. "If you guys need anything while I am away, Dylan should be able to help you." She ceremoniously stood up and walked toward the door, then sat down at one of the chairs at the back of the room.

"It's 11:01," Chris said.

"Ugh, not the time again," Boris moaned.

"After reviewing logs, Harmony sees successful two-factor authentications for several of the users who had suspicious activity. It turns out that the user's child had their phone and clicked Accept on the two-factor request."

"Brent, can we please initiate our compromised user workflow and lock those accounts," Dylan said.

"You got it, boss," Brent said, nodding.

"Hi, Harmony, it's Luis again. It's 11:12 and we've detected some port-scanning activity originating from the treadmill firmware update server. We believe this started around 10:30."

"Do we think that the update server could have been used to compromise the treadmills having issues?" Kim asked, looking between Noor and Boris.

"That's a possibility," Boris admitted.

"How do we find out?" Kim asked.

"We don't have a dashboard or anything like we talked about. We'd have to run a report manually to see when the last firmware change was made."

"Should we take the server down, boss?" Harmony asked.

"Let's take it off the network," Dylan said nodding. "But let's keep it running so we can preserve any evidence that the attacker might have left behind."

"It's now 11:45 and it appears that protesters have begun to arrive and are gathering near the front gate of the building," Chris said, turning the page in his notebook and scrolling down the page on his computer.

"How many protesters?" Kim asked.

"Currently there are about twenty-five people gathered, but they are starting to interfere with employees leaving the building coming to and from lunch," Chris said.

"Should we call the police?" Vic asked. "Don't they need a permit or something?"

"We can call, but I don't think it will look good if the police start arresting protesters," April said, leaning forward.

"We've gotten an update," Chris said. "It appears that the media is now onsite setting up satellite trucks outside the building to cover the protest."

"April, let's prepare a statement for the press," Vic said, standing up to grab a pitcher of water. He poured another glass of water for himself. "We can invite them inside and tell them we take these allegations seriously and that we will investigate and resolve any issues we find."

"Yes, I can do that," April said.

"I'll have some more security staff positioned outside the gate to direct traffic to keep the protesters from blocking traffic," Kim said.

"It's now 12:25," Chris said. "In reviewing traffic logs, the network team sees successful connections from the update server to another server . . . the network vulnerability scanning server."

"Oh, crud," Harmony said.

"Let's take the server off the network asap," Dylan said. "I think we're officially in a high-severity incident. We should send notifications to all IT staff to be on alert. They should review their logs and log off any remote users they can identify. We should bring in our incident response partner."

"I'll contact them and bring them up to speed," Rose said.

"We need a list of any network traffic that the vulnerability server has made in the last twenty-four hours."

"I'll work on that," Harmony said.

"It's now 12:45," Chris said. "After receiving the notification to be on high alert, several IT staff reported noticing a drone flying around outside the building. It has now been hovering for several minutes outside the northwest corner of the second floor of the building.

"It is 1 p.m.," Chris continued. "After Vic gave a briefing to the press, the crowd of about twenty-five people began to disperse. The drone also is seen moving away from the building as the crowd leaves, but it isn't possible to see which person retrieved the drone as they left."

"I don't understand," Vic said, folding his arms. "What could the drone have done? Just gotten video from inside the building?"

"It's possible someone had written things on a whiteboard. The drone could have seen passwords or product specifications." Rose shrugged. The group broke into several smaller conversations as people speculated what data could have been observed by a drone looking into the building.

"It's now 1:05," Chris said, looking around the room to get everyone's attention. The group quieted down, focusing back on him. "Harmony reports that the scanning server was able to connect to nearly every server and client in the organization during the last three hours. It downloaded some unique malware to one client in particular."

"Let's get that client off the network, please, Harmony," Dylan said.

"Already on it," Harmony reported, tapping the keyboard on her laptop to pretend she was making a change.

"After investigating," Chris said, "Harmony identifies the specific computer. It is located in the northwest corner of the building on the second floor."

Dylan was the first to speak up. "Let's get the computer into the hands of our incident response firm to see if they can identify what that 'unique' malware actually was and how it got past our EDR tool."

"It's now the next day," Chris said. "Your incident response firm reports that the malware was a data exfiltration tool. It used the LED on the computer to flash rapidly. They've only ever seen this used by sophisticated nation-state attackers. They report that it is possible that data could have been transmitted to the drone." The group gasped at this announcement. Several of the department heads around the table seemed skeptical of this.

"How do we know what data could have been stolen?" Kim asked.

Kofi spoke up for the first time. "We definitely need to know what data was stolen to decide what to do next. We might need to do victim notifications or file a report with the SEC depending on what the answer to that is. How do we tell?"

"Our incident response firm would have made a forensically secure copy of the client drive and can review what data is being stored in memory," Dylan said. "We can scan the device, but that may take several days."

"We'll need to notify our cyber insurance carrier to let them know we've had an incident," Kim said.

"No," Kofi interrupted. "We don't have enough evidence yet to know that there has been a breach. We aren't required to notify unless there is a breach. And the legal definition of a breach is when data is lost. We aren't required to notify anyone yet."

"We know there's been an incident," Dylan said.

"We don't know if anything was stolen," Kofi countered. This was true, but it still bothered Dylan.

"We'll examine the PC that was in view of the drone," Dylan said. "If there was any data exfiltrated, it would have had to pass through there. If there was any data on that device, I think we'd have to assume that it was compromised. Same with any other system. We have to assume accounts on those devices were compromised as well."

"How long do we wait?" Kim asked. "What if that analysis takes a month? Or more?"

"That would be a nightmare," April said.

"Every step matters," said a voice from the back of the room. It was Olivia. She had somehow managed to walk in when Dylan wasn't looking. She was standing up now. "Kofi, our response should take that into account. We do right by our customers because it matters." He sat back in his chair and nodded. Kofi might not have liked it, but Olivia did still have a large ownership stake in the company.

"If we had an incident and we didn't notify our carrier," Kim calmly explained, "then that could be grounds enough for them to deny a claim against our cyber insurance. Especially if it looks like we didn't have adequate controls in place."

The group continued to discuss the incident response process for several more hours until they reached the end of the scenario. Vic was the first to speak. "Thank you, Chris, Dylan, Noor, and the Project Zero Trust team. This was certainly eye opening and I think we all learned a tremendous amount today. Now I totally expect that you'll make sure this scenario never plays out again in real life." Nigel hooted at this, and the group broke into applause. Harmony and Rose high-fived as the meeting started to break apart and the attendees started to leave.

Dylan stood up and announced, "For the folks invited to the hotwash, let's regroup in five. For the folks going to the afterparty, don't start without us!"

Agent Smecker walked to Dylan and firmly shook his hand. "I just wanted to say, that was a real firefight." Dylan stared as the FBI agent then slipped out the door and made his way down the stairs.

Kofi patted Dylan on the back and took his hand. "Dylan, we've got an opening for our monthly poker tournament. You play?"

"Um, yeah. Yes, I've played a hand or two."

"Good. We play Texas hold 'em."

Dylan walked with Kofi to the door. As he came back, Kim was walking back in with a cup of coffee. Noor had taken her jacket off and was discussing something quietly with Rose and Boris. Chris was sitting on the desk scrolling through his phone. Peter was still on the video wall looking offscreen as though he were looking at a second monitor.

"So why do we call this thing a hotwash?" Boris asked.

"It comes from the military," Kim said. "When I was in the Army, we'd sometimes use really hot water to rinse our weapons to remove the grit and larger particles. This made it easier to clean up later. A lot of folks from the military end up in emergency management and security, so the term stuck. It's just a debrief meeting, but we want to hang on to all the important lessons learned while they're still fresh in our memory."

"Thanks for staying a bit late today," Dylan said. "Our goal will be to capture any action items and prioritize issues. We should track and report the issues we found. We still need to report on value back to the business."

"We also should debrief what went right so we can duplicate our successes," Noor added.

"I'm going to get PTSD every time I hear someone announce what time it is from now on," Boris said.

"You all did a terrific job," Peter said. "You might not have gotten a sense of how challenging it was to move through the network because you only saw when I successfully got into a system, but I'm not kidding when I say it was a real challenge to get around inside the network."

"You made it look easy," Boris said.

"Keep in mind that this exercise took months of planning," Chris said. "Peter had full access to find weaknesses and knew your environment from the ransomware incident. Also, the SOC was able to detect a lot of his activity very quickly after it happened."

"What are some things that we could have done better?" Noor asked.

"I recommend that you consider using a memory-safe IoT programming language like Rust," Peter said. "IoT devices typically don't have a lot of horsepower, so they're very susceptible to buffer overflows, for example. From the other penetration testers that I've talked to, this has had a huge impact for their other clients. It's almost eliminated all the most common ways we exploit IoT devices."

"Excellent suggestion," Boris said. "We've already programmed the new 360Tread in Rust, but we will definitely prioritize migrating the TreadMarch platform to Rust."

"I also noticed that a lot of the IoT devices were all open to one another. I didn't have time to pursue it, but I saw there were some printers that were reachable," Peter said.

"Why is that a big deal?" Kim asked, taking another drink from her coffee.

"Some printers have hard drives built in and store all the files that were printed or scanned by those devices," Peter explained. "Those should be locked down. It was out of scope for this engagement, but you should also look at your equipment recycling program to make sure you're wiping devices before they leave your control."

"Zero Trust computer recycling. I like it," Dylan said.

"I also noticed that after I owned the update server, there were several servers where I could have forced them to downgrade their security to a vulnerable protocol," Peter said. "This is common where organizations are concerned about backward compatibility, but I'd recommend not allowing downgrade."

"How do we do that?" Kim asked.

"I'd recommend disabling support for SSL 3.0," Peter said. "Also, don't allow anything prior to TLS 1.2."

"That sounds easy," Kim said.

"We had a project to get rid of TLS 1.1 a couple years ago, but it keeps popping back up as an issue," Noor said. "We'll get on top of that; that seems like a pretty high priority."

"I also noticed that there were some vulnerable libraries on the servers I was able to connect to," Peter said. "I decided not to go that direction in the interest of time since the vulnerability scanner being open was a more surefire route. But you should definitely be able to quickly identify open source software dependencies in your environment."

"What do we do about the vulnerability scanning server?" Dylan asked.

"Segmentation isn't really a great option for scanners since they need to be able to talk to everything," Peter said. "When you're using credentialed scans, you don't need all those ports open, so you can just lock them down. But if you're doing uncredentialed scans, only keep those firewall rules open when you're running the scan and remove them when you're done. Or set those rules to only apply during a specific schedule during the week."

"What's a credentialed scan?" Kim asked.

"There are two ways of scanning," Chris explained. "You can scan for open ports from the outside, like looking for open windows or doors to a house. This can help simulate what a cybercriminal would see, but there can be a lot of false positives. A credentialed scan means we have the keys to the house and can go inside to make sure the house is locked up tight."

"What about the request to build a treadmill dashboard from Vic in the beginning?" Dylan asked.

"I think that's an interesting idea," Boris said. "We will add it to our roadmap, but as far as priorities go it's lower on our list than some of the code improvements we've talked about."

"Was the drone thing at the end real?" Kim asked.

"Yes. We have seen some clever exfiltration techniques over the years," Peter said. "Just taking over the flashing LED on a computer can be used to download data at about 4Kbps. The drone needs to be less than one hundred feet from the LED."

"So we need to install curtains?" Dylan asked.

Peter laughed. "We included the drone to get you thinking about all the alternative ways that data can leave. I saw a demo once where a researcher used the memory bus of a computer as an antenna by amplifying the transmission of data between the motherboard and memory. This was effective at about 1 Kbps at over one hundred feet. But a threat actor can always just plant a burner cell phone inside the building to exfiltrate data."

Dylan and Rose walked down the stairs to the basement. They walked under the banner that read "Abandon All Trusts, Ye Who Enter." Harmony, Rose, Isabelle, Noor, and Olivia were all seated around the table in front of the projector. Olivia and Harmony were sitting together on the green couch. Brent was in the corner making popcorn in a real live popcorn maker. Nigel bagged the popcorn and began handing it out.

Harmony had placed several additional large monitors around the center projection screen. They were all paused on different news videos from different networks. They were all covering the arrest of 3nc0r3.

As Dylan and Noor entered, Harmony pressed play and all of the streams started playing simultaneously, but only the audio from the main projection screen played.

A man in a suit came on the screen holding a microphone outside the café where Rose had been the day before. He held his finger to his earpiece and nodded before he began speaking. "This is Brian Fantana coming to you live from the scene where authorities have arrested twenty-nine-year-old Richard Greyson, who they believe to be the cybercriminal Encore."

The screen shifted from the live view of the reporter to some recorded footage as the reporter continued narrating. They showed a man with a jacket over his head being led into the back of a police car. "The FBI had set up a sting for the self-described hacker and were able to trace payments made during the sting to Greyson's bitcoin wallet. Greyson faces felony cybercrime charges in at least three countries."

The screen shifted to the exterior of the MarchFit headquarters building, focusing on the logo of the building as the reporter continued. "MarchFit confirms that Richard Greyson had actually applied to work for the company several years ago but was turned down for the job. The company declined to comment further."

The video shifted back to a view of the reporter outside the café where Agent Smecker was standing behind an impromptu lectern where several microphones had been put in place. Just at the very edge of the screen, Rose was standing, arms folded, still looking at where Greyson was locked in the police cruiser.

"The FBI would like to thank all of the agencies that came together to make this arrest possible," Smecker said. "But most of all, we'd like to thank MarchFit for their cooperation. The Bureau relies on information from the community to help stop cybercriminals wherever they are."

The video changed again to the exterior of the police cruiser as it was pulling away from the café with Greyson inside. The jacket covering his face had fallen away, revealing a thin man with a thick mop of curly hair. The window to the cruiser was down, and as he was being led away, Mr. Greyson could be heard saying, "I can't believe I trusted her." He said it in perfect English.

"Wait," Harmony said. "When he Zoom-bombed us, he was faking a European accent to throw us off?"

The news anchor came back on the screen and wondered aloud, "Who is this mysterious woman? We may never know."

The Project Zero Trust team knew. They cheered, "Rose! Rose! Rose!"

Key Takeaways

Like most things in cybersecurity, the model for how to conduct a successful tabletop exercise can be found in a NIST Standard. For tabletop exercises, the NIST Special Publication is 800-84. This standard defines a number of key considerations when building your own tabletop exercises. To start, you'll need to define the objectives of the exercise before you start building the scenario. You'll also want to take into account the audience for the exercise to ensure that the right people are in the room to accomplish your goals. The Master Scenario Events List (MSEL) will be the guide the moderator uses to keep the tabletop exercise on track. A sample MESL is included as Appendix C.

Tabletop exercises are critical to any good security program. Just like every commercial building in the country is required to conduct a fire drill, businesses should regularly test their incident response plans in a simulated fashion. This helps every team member who may be involved in a real incident to understand what their role is on the team and gives them a safe way to practice. Conducting a tabletop also helps improve the incident response plan by evaluating whether the plan would be effective in different scenarios and whether employees will be able to follow the plan.

There are a number of different ways to conduct a tabletop exercise. In its most basic form, team members from across the organization can be in the room to discuss an organization's response to a breach scenario. Usually a moderator walks the team through a timeline of events, and the group will discuss their collective responses to various moves and injects. In this case, MarchFit decided to perform a more complex type of tabletop, known as a live-fire drill. A live-fire exercise will involve penetration testers performing their own activity in coordination with the moderator.

Typically, tabletop exercises will involve leaders from throughout the business alongside technology professionals. This can help business leaders understand some of the challenges that the organizations face and will help build connections between different departments. Communication during an event is critical, so having trust relationships already created during these exercises is very helpful. Some more technical exercises can include only IT staff. A more technical exercise can help break down barriers inside the IT team by helping everyone see the big picture of what happens during an incident response and the different roles people need to play and what the proper procedures are.

Tabletop exercises are a big part of the Zero Trust design methodology step: monitor and maintain. A tabletop exercise can help make IT teams more efficient during a real event. Sometimes teams will discover that they aren't receiving the right logs or that the technology environment has changed. Tabletop exercises can help test your controls as well, and can help identify when the SOC isn't getting the data they need to be able to respond effectively. The more effective an IT team is, the faster a breach is contained and it will take less time to recover.

Even though MarchFit had nearly completed the initial phase of their Zero Trust journey when they conducted their tabletop exercise, there were still ways for a threat actor to get access to their systems. The first method that the penetration tester used to get into the MarchFit network was to exploit the trust relationship that the company had with their own treadmills. The treadmills are an example of an Internet of Things (IoT) device, and cybercriminals will commonly compromise these types of devices because they don't have all of the protections that other devices may have. Once the tester took over a treadmill, they got access to an internal update server in the MarchFit network and were able to move laterally from there.

The other trust relationship that the penetration tester chose to exploit was in the security team's tools. Many organizations use vulnerability scanners to identify devices that are vulnerable to attack. There are two types of scans that these devices will run. The first is a port scan for each target that is used to probe what applications might be installed on a device, to fingerprint what operating system is running, and to determine if those match any known vulnerabilities. The other type of scan, a credentialed scan, uses real usernames and passwords to log in to a device to directly check what software is running. The credentialed scan yields much more accurate results, but many organizations will open holes in firewalls for these scanners to talk to everything in the network no matter what kind of scan is being run. In effect, this means that a vulnerability scanning server is highly trusted, which makes it an attractive target for attack.

In the exercise, there were also a number of events that didn't have anything to do with the attack that the penetration tester was performing. We called these injects into the scenario *red herrings*. The term red herring comes from a story where a man distracted dogs chasing a rabbit with some strong-smelling fish. We often find ourselves receiving conflicting information during an incident. Experts call this phenomena the fog of war. Our brains will naturally start to connect the dots to draw conclusions, but often we don't have all the information we need to create a clear picture. The best way to combat the fog of war is to communicate, ask questions, be transparent, but most of all, don't stick with your conclusions when you receive new information.

This exercise reinforced the trust the business leaders put in the team. By practicing, we understand better what our roles should be and how we can best help. Conducting this exercise after their ransomware event gives the team a chance to show how much more prepared they are. This can also help leaders be better advocates for security initiatives since they'll have seen firsthand what it takes to respond to an event. And because these exercises are done in a safe environment, it's okay for people to make mistakes. We want to be able to learn from those mistakes in a controlled environment where there aren't any consequences rather than during a real event.

But don't just do tabletop exercises for executives or IT teams. Many additional departments in an organization can benefit from practicing what might happen for common events like ransomware, business email compromise, or phishing. These conversations can lead to potential improvements when they are combined with a Zero Trust implementation because we can look for potential opportunities to remove trust from digital systems.

Chapter 11
Every Step Matters

The reporter tucked her earpiece back into her ear. The noise of tens of thousands of people echoing around the exhibit hall was almost deafening, but she could hear her producer clearly in her earpiece. Behind her were the flashing lights of a technology booth with the MarchFit logo clearly displayed over her shoulder. She adjusted her dark hair back into place and held her microphone out in front of her. The cameraman counted down from three, and she began her opening, "Hi, this is Monica Stuart reporting to you live from the massive Consumer Electronics Show, the biggest technology event in the world. And stealing all the headlines of the show this year? MarchFit. I'm here with Olivia Reynolds, founder of MarchFit. Olivia, I don't think anyone was expecting what you had in store for us."

The camera turned so that both Monica and Olivia were now in the shot. Olivia was already holding her own microphone. "I'm thrilled to be here," Olivia said. "The last six months have been some of the hardest times in my life. But seeing how excited people are for our new gaming treadmill makes me feel like it was all worth it."

"The world wants to know: Are you a gamer?" Monica asked.

Olivia laughed. "I have to admit that I've been playing Elden Ring entirely on our new treadmill at the office for a few months. Running around killing monsters for an hour is my new favorite workout."

"Take us through a tour of how the treadmill works," Monica said, as the camera turned again to show the MarchFit booth. There were sixteen treadmills arranged in a square, each occupied by a gamer wearing a VR headset. A line extended halfway across the exhibit hall with people waiting their turn to play.

Each treadmill had a pole extending from the side of the base to about seven feet in the air. The players wore harnesses that were hung from the pole to keep them from falling over. The players were running, jumping, or dodging from side to side as they swung their arms. The treadmill closest to the camera had changed shape slightly so that the player appeared to be running up a hill.

"The treadmills allow for full 360-degree motion and integrate fully with the player's motion in the game," Olivia explained. "As you can see, they can simulate going over different types of terrain thanks to the internal arms inside the treadmill." There was a video playing behind Olivia that showed a cross section of the treadmill to show how each of the arms inside the treadmill could move independently from one another. "We already integrate with all the different VR platforms, but for those who prefer a more traditional experience, we also integrate with PCs thanks to our quad curved gaming monitors," she said, pointing to a treadmill surrounded by monitors where a pro European player was playing FIFA.

"Well, I'll let you go since it looks like you've got a lot of people that want your attention," Monica said, gesturing to executives from Activision, Microsoft, Nintendo, EA, and Sony who had gathered around them waiting for their turn to talk to Olivia. Olivia's assistant led her back to one of the meeting areas on the second story of the booth and the executives all followed, hoping to get their turn. Monica gestured to the cameraman, and they began to break down their gear to move on to their next interview.

Hours later, Olivia walked out of the meeting to look over the balcony of their booth. Dylan was there drinking a coffee. "Hey, it's good to see you again. I still feel bad that you were forced out as CEO. I wish there was something I could have done."

"Are you kidding?" Olivia said. "It was the best thing that could have happened. I'm an engineer and an inventor first. It was the right time to hand off the role to someone who could focus on running the company. Now I get to spend my time doing what I love, which is building new things."

"That's really cool," Dylan admitted, remembering all the tools in her office. "I had no idea what I was in for, but I'm glad I stuck it out."

"I didn't know what I was getting into when I started the company! I felt like I had to be both Jobs and Wozniak. But now that I've gone through it, I think I'm more like Woz."

"Really? I always thought of you more as a Hedy Lamarr type." Dylan said.

"The important thing was to make sure the product launch happened," Olivia said. "Hey, are you busy right now?"

"I was just about to walk around and check out some of the new products on the floor," Dylan said.

"Oh, sorry. You won't have time for that. The folks from the gaming companies wanted to talk to you about Zero Trust. They want to know how we turned our security around so quickly. I think they were more excited to talk to you than they were about talking to me," she said, opening the door to the meeting room for him.

Several days later, Dylan sat down at his desk. It felt like the first time he'd actually been in his own office since he started at MarchFit. He had a window overlooking the lobby of the building and could see the wire mesh shoes running down the center of the corridor. He started his next Zoom meeting early so he wouldn't forget, then began unpacking the cardboard box he had brought from home but hadn't yet had time to unpack. He pulled out a painting his daughter had painted for him when she was a child and placed it on his desk. Dylan continued unpacking until Aaron joined the call. "Dylan, nice to hear from you," he said as his video came online.

"You still owe me one last phone call," Dylan said. "I thought it would be nice to do a video chat since things have settled down and our Zero Trust project has wrapped up."

"Wrapped up?" Aaron asked.

"We finished up the project just in time for the new product launch just like we had planned," Dylan said.

"Oh, man, that's good to hear. But you're definitely not done." Aaron laughed.

"Did I miss a step?" Dylan asked. "We went through all our protect surfaces and used the design methodology to tailor our controls. I mean I get that it's a continuous process, but. . ."

"It seems like I may have forgotten to mention the Zero Trust Maturity Model," Aaron said apologetically.

"I thought we were going to do Zero Trust in six months?" Dylan asked. "How long will the rest of the process take?"

"We didn't just pick the six-month time frame because MarchFit had a product launch coming up," Aaron explained. "We picked the six-month time frame because of the natural business cycle. I recommend to all of our clients that we focus our efforts into six- to nine-month initiatives. We do that for a few reasons, but the biggest one is because of the corporate budget cycle. When we get budget allocated for our projects we have to be able to show value based on that budget allocation. If we started with a three-or five-year campaign, we'd lose funding halfway through the project and the initiative would get abandoned because we couldn't show any return on the business's investment."

"That makes sense," Dylan admitted.

"Because Zero Trust is a strategic initiative," Aaron explained, "it's important to benchmark your Zero Trust journey and measure your maturity over time. We designed the maturity model based on the standard Capability Maturity Model, which has five stages: initial, repeatable, defined, managed, and optimized. For each protect surface, the Zero Trust Maturity Model measures the maturity of each stage of the design methodology."

"So we need to baseline our level of maturity for each of our protect surfaces, and the next step would be to select goals for improving each of those areas?" Dylan guessed.

"That's right. But keep in mind you'll always need to be strategic with what areas you want to focus on improving. The priority will always align with March-Fit's priorities and the specific risks you're facing," Aaron said.

"Does that mean it's OK to not be as mature in some less-critical areas?" Dylan asked, pulling out a snow globe from the box and placing it on his desk. Inside was a picture of Dylan and his daughter from a summer vacation.

"You'll have to go through that rightsizing exercise to make sure you've got the resources you need to deliver the right level of security. You don't need to have the same level of maturity for each step in the design methodology or for every protect surface. But starting with the baseline can help you show how and where you're investing in security and how that aligns with the business."

"That seems like it would become really complicated to explain," Dylan admitted.

"I like using the transaction flow matrix chart that John Kindervag developed to help show how protect surface policies are developed to talk internally. Here, let me share my screen."

"The transaction flow matrix can help you understand how each of the different protect surfaces can potentially impact one another. As you think about the maturity of your protect surfaces, you'll need to think about how the blast radius from a compromise in one might impact the other protect surfaces."

"You're saying that we can't think about any protect surface in a vacuum?" Dylan said.

"Exactly," Aaron confirmed. "But you only have so many IT resources. So if you had ten team members and eight of them are tied up working on firewall rules because of all the complexity of your rules, then you might be sacrificing control over identities or visibility into logs, for example."

"What do you think we should work on next?" Dylan asked.

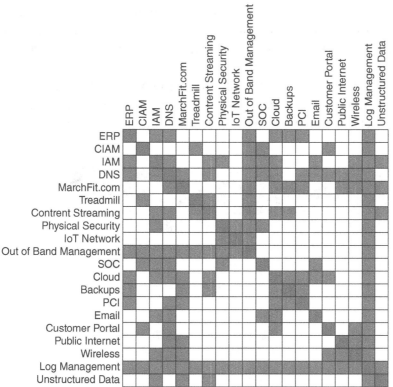

Transaction Flow Map One—All the protect surfaces are defined, and the transaction flow matrix can show which protect surfaces are allowed to communicate with one another.

"I've got a few ideas. If I were you I'd be looking into continuous flow mapping using BAS—breach and attack simulation—or emulation tools. I'd also be looking carefully at deception technologies."

"I've never heard of breach and attack simulation," Dylan admitted.

"Not many organizations have complete testing infrastructures where they can detonate malware and test whether all their controls are adequate," Aaron explained. "BAS or emulation software helps do this kind of testing in more of a real-time way than doing an extended security assessment or penetration test. I think it's most beneficial for more mature organizations. Breach and attack simulation can simulate how a real attacker might attempt to attack an organization using predefined attack paths. With emulation, the tools help customize how attacks are launched, using threat intelligence to contextualize how the business actually works."

"What makes you say we should look at deception?" Dylan asked.

"With Zero Trust, we've focused on removing all the trusts we can in order to make our networks more secure. But with deception, we can selectively add trusts back into the network using lures, beacons, breadcrumbs, and decoys. The idea is that Zero Trust can conceal real data while revealing fake trusted sources to distract, delay, or detect threat actors. I know we've talked about the MITRE ATT&CK framework in the past, but they also have something called the Engage framework. Let me show you," Aaron said, pulling up the MITRE Engage framework.

Prepare	Expose		Affect			Elicit		Understand
Plan	Collect	Detect	Prevent	Direct	Disrupt	Reassure	Motivate	Analyze
Cyber Threat Intelligence	API Monitoring	Introduced Vulnerabilities	Baseline	Attack Vector Migration	Isolation	Application Diversity	Application Diversity	After-Action Review
Engagement Environment	Network Monitoring	Lures	Hardware Manipulation	Email Manipulation	Lures	Artifact Diversity	Artifact Diversity	Cyber Threat Intelligence
Gating Criteria	Software Manipulation	Malware Detonation	Isolation	Introduced Vulnerabilities	Network Manipulation	Burn-In	Information Manipulation	Threat Model
Operational Objective	System Activity Monitoring	Network Analysis	Network Manipulation	Lures	Software Manipulation	Email Manipulation	Introduced Vulnerabilities	
Persona Creation			Security Controls	Malware Detonation		Information Manipulation	Malware Detonation	
Storyboarding				Network Manipulation		Network Diversity	Network Diversity	
Threat Model				Peripheral Management		Peripheral Management	Personas	
				Security Controls		Pocket Litter		
				Software Manipulation				

MITRE Engage Matrix—The Engage Matrix depicts five stages of creating an active defense to disrupt cyberattacks using deception technologies.

"The MITRE ATT&CK Framework provides an analysis of all the TTPs of attacker behavior so that defenders can better understand and defend against those TTPs," Aaron explained. "The Engage Matrix is a framework for defenders to help them to provide an active defense against attackers. The idea isn't to just passively defend, it is to proactively engage attackers to bring the fight to them."

"Does that mean we're going to hack back?" Dylan asked.

"No, as far as I know hacking back is still illegal," Aaron said. "But using tools like deception can get inside the heads of our adversaries."

"How does that work?" Dylan asked.

"The first principle of Zero Trust is to remove all trust relationships from digital systems," Aaron said. "With the Engage Matrix, we build profiles of threat actors that target us, and carefully expose specific resources that act like breadcrumbs that lead the attacker toward lures or honeypots. The next phase is to expose what the attackers are after with those breadcrumbs. Then we disrupt the attacker, what they have visibility into, and what actions they may take next. We induce them to show us what their toolkits look like and we use that to help us better understand their capabilities. That feeds into the threat intel pipeline and helps us improve the controls we have on our protect surfaces."

"I've always heard that honeypots can attract unwanted attention," Dylan said.

"I'm not recommending that you set up a honeypot that's exposed to the Internet," Aaron said. "That will be too noisy to provide any real value. But it's been shown that when threat actors know that you're using deception technologies in your network, the bad guys spend less time inside your network."

"It's like when a burglar hears a siren in the distance and worries that it's the police coming for them," Dylan said.

"That's right. The NSA actually had some pen testers attempt to get into different networks, but when they told them they were using deception technologies, the red teams started to doubt their own tools and questioned whether the targets they were finding that had weaknesses were actually decoys. This effect persisted even when the NSA wasn't actually using deception."

"Like when people put a home alarm monitoring company sign on their house but don't actually have an alarm," Dylan said.

"Exactly. In a way, we're taking advantage of the trust relationship that the attackers have with their own tools or their own telemetry. Deception brings the fight to the mind of the adversary. We're getting inside their heads to disrupt attacks," Aaron explained.

"Well, I guess we still have a lot of work to do," Dylan said.

"Good luck, Dylan. Let's definitely grab lunch and catch up the next time I'm in town!" Aaron said.

Dylan had just finished the call when Noor knocked on the door to his office and stepped in. "I don't think I've ever seen you in your office before," she said.

"I've figured that if I'm in my office, I'm not doing my job," he said with a laugh. "It's been going from one meeting to another and making sure everyone on the team has everything they need." He pushed his chair away from his desk so he wouldn't be distracted by his computer.

"Do you mind if I sit?" Dylan nodded and she sat down. She saw the picture of the girl on Dylan's desk. "I didn't know you had a daughter."

"Oh, yeah. She's in college now. She wants to be a veterinarian one day, but we'll see if that changes by the time she's done," he said, smiling warmly.

"I've got some good news," Noor said, smiling. "As you know, I've been serving both as MarchFit's CIO and as our CISO. I talked to Vic and Donna, and we all agree that it's time that we hired our first dedicated CISO."

"That's fantastic news," Dylan said.

"Well, given your experience, we were hoping that you might be interested in the role," Noor said.

"Me?" Dylan said.

"Take some time to think about it," Noor said. "No rush this time. I would like you to get some security certifications in the first year on the job. We would be willing to send you to an executive CISO leadership institute to help you continue to develop your skills as well. But you don't have to say yes now."

Dylan was standing at the projection screen inside ZTC. He was outlining the next phase of Project Zero Trust after reviewing the maturity model. Harmony, Rose, Isabelle, and Nigel were sitting at their seats watching his presentation when there was a knock at the door. Harmony turned out the lights, then flipped a switch that turned on some colored disco lights. Brent came into the briefing center pushing a cart with a giant trophy on it.

"Guys, you didn't have to do this," Dylan said.

"We all got trophies too," Harmony said, passing out small trophies to all the team members.

"We're gonna have to change the codes to the briefing center," Dylan said, seeing that the trophies had been 3D printed.

"Don't you dare," Brent said. "I get ninety percent of my coffee intake from that espresso machine."

"How much coffee do you drink?" Rose asked.

"Not coffee. Espresso," Brent said. "And for your information," he said to Dylan, "that's not a trophy. It's a cake." And Brent produced a giant kitchen knife and proceeded to cut into the trophy.

"It's just like that show on Netflix, *Is It Cake*!" Isabelle squealed. "The base even looks like wood with that grain." The trophy had a plaque at the bottom that read: "Zero Trust Champion 2022: Dylan Thomas."

They stopped the meeting to eat the cake. It was delicious.

"I'm gonna need to build a pretty good security team," Dylan said as the others finished their cake. "You guys know anyone who wants to work for a brand-new CISO?" he asked.

"I think you've already got a pretty good team," Rose said. Although everyone's mouths were full, murmurs of agreement came from around the room.

"Aw, guys. I didn't want to assume that you'd want to move over to the new team," Dylan said.

"And leave all this cake for someone else?" Harmony said. "Forget it."

"Well, it's not just going to be us. We'll have to do some recruiting as well," Dylan said.

Several months later Dylan was standing in front of a group of new members of his security team on the steps to the executive briefing center. He put his hand on the metal shoe that was halfway up the stairs. The group followed him up the stairs and stood underneath the giant shoe.

Dylan spoke up and said, "Turn around and take a look at MarchFit's motto just above the entrance to the building." The group turned around and Dylan continued speaking. "The first thing that I want you all to know is that we're not measured on whether we are hacked or not," he said. "We're measured on how we respond to those challenges. We're measured on whether we rise to the challenge. Every step matters."

Key Takeaways

One of the biggest obstacles to improving security for organizations today is that there are so many technology silos. Some teams only support antivirus products or firewalls. Other teams do database encryption or application security. Some teams support identity. Other teams do cloud security. Some teams report to a CIO, whereas others report to a CTO or CISO. These silos prevent collaboration and communication. I believe that a Zero Trust strategy can help break down these silos and help unify teams around a singular focus: preventing or containing data breaches. This is why *Project Zero Trust* brought together a team of diverse individuals from throughout MarchFit—to break down these barriers and help the organization evolve.

When I started my own Zero Trust journey, I didn't take into account whether I'd be able to scale our implementation of microsegmentation and other controls along with the size of the team that I had at the time. We were extremely granular in our controls in order to contain the blast radius of any incident. But because we didn't start with the concept of protect surfaces, we applied the same level of focus and control everywhere. As a result, our controls became too complex to manage. I believe that John Kindervag's Zero Trust Design Principles and Methodology can drastically reduce the complexity in your approach to Zero Trust.

The only way to be successful at implementing Zero Trust is to build a team. Success starts with support at the highest levels of your organization. Zero Trust will require changes, and those changes will require you to collaborate with different business leaders throughout your organization to both understand how the business functions and coordinate security with how the business uses technology.

But you also need a team in IT. Most of the changes that are required to support Zero Trust won't necessarily be done by security teams. Dylan's team was made up of people from all over IT who supported security. Much of the work that will be required will be done by infrastructure teams that support networks or servers. We included examples of how application owners and software developers are also a part of the process to limit trust in how their systems work. Zero Trust projects that bring together diverse teams help break down silos and allow for streamlined collaboration. MarchFit created an Identity Governance group and an Enterprise Architecture Group and had mature project management to ensure that the Zero Trust initiatives were completed in a reasonable time period and that these changes would be sustained as the business continued to grow and change.

Zero Trust requires you to have the basics in place. One of the first places you should start is with an inventory. In order to protect something, you need to know where it is, how it works, and what it needs to talk to. In Zero Trust, there is no concept of unknown traffic. If it is unknown, it is blocked by default. The next step in Zero Trust requires you to prioritize your efforts. Having done a business impact assessment is helpful because this document will measure the impact to the business for each service in the organization. To know what applications are the crown jewels, you can look to this document. In addition, every organization needs to have a technology risk register to have a current list of the biggest threats to the business from a technology perspective. A risk register should include much more than vulnerabilities; it can document lack of capabilities in specific areas and identify single points of failure or weaknesses in the various controls that the organization has in place.

Having the basics helps speed along the process, but if those basics aren't already in place, launching a Zero Trust project can help your organization build out your inventory, risk register, CMDB, and business continuity plans along the way.

An organization can't have cybersecurity without good physical security. We chose physical security as one of the learning protect surfaces because it is so often overlooked when it comes to security. Often, organizations outsource security guard duties to third parties. The physical security technologies like card readers and cameras are also often outsourced. Without internal oversight, these organizations will focus on keeping these systems operational without regard for the security of those systems. Although an organization can bring in partners to help with physical security, organizations can't outsource the responsibility and accountability for security.

In the beginning, we started by understanding the business. The Project Zero Trust team worked on several practice and learning protect surfaces so that they were prepared to fully implement Zero Trust when they got to the crown jewels of the organization: the ERP system. Because the ERP system is so critical to the business, the team was also exposed to several different departments to better understand how the business operates. ERP systems today are often a blind spot to security teams; they don't receive ERP logs, perform vulnerability scans, or review code changes prior to being deployed in production. These challenges are critical for any protect surface, but ERP systems may require specialized tools to accomplish this task.

Identity is the cornerstone of Zero Trust. Identity is both a protect surface and a critical control. The identity system needs to be protected better than almost any other protect surface because of its criticality to an organization. Consumer Identity and Access Management is your outward-facing identity surface and should be separated from your employee and privileged account management platforms. But Zero Trust also consumes identity—many of the controls that Zero Trust employs rely on identity to be effective. This is so true that the NIST standard for Zero Trust (NIST SP 800-207) focuses on identity to drive Zero Trust deployments.

Many organizations that develop their own software have adopted a DevOps philosophy to help them focus on the business. DevOps helps organizations deliver better software more quickly, and this development pipeline can include security testing that can ensure that trust relationships, like embedded passwords, emails, or IP addresses, are removed from code before being released into production.

The SOC plays a huge role in Zero Trust because of their unique view of an organization. The SOC correlates strongly with the monitor and maintain phase of the Zero Trust design methodology, and whether the SOC is run inside an organization or is run by an MSSP, the SOC should provide continuous feedback on the state of an organization. Rather than simply viewing alerts and escalating them back to an organization, a Zero Trust SOC can help improve controls inside an organization to reduce false positives and help identify opportunities for improvement. Maintaining an internal 24x7 SOC is probably outside the capabilities of most organizations. Working with an MSSP service that can help tailor their monitoring to meet your business needs is crucial. But you also need an MSSP that can align with your own protect surfaces, incorporate data from penetration testing findings, and integrate with your specialized internal tools.

Many organizations have chosen to leverage cloud services to help improve their scalability. The cloud, however, isn't just one protect surface; it's many different ones. One of the best ways to ensure that Zero Trust processes are followed in the cloud is to have strong IT governance controls in place, like a Project Management Office to enforce that consistent controls are in place to protect cloud-based services. To protect something, you have to be able to see it. Unlike for on-premises services, there is limited visibility into cloud services, so additional tools like WAFs, CASBs, or API monitoring are needed. In addition, because cloud services necessarily involve third parties, organizations need to have strong contract and third-party vendor management processes in place to manage the risk of a third party having a breach.

People play a critical role in the success of Zero Trust. Most security practitioners will tell you that security is made up of people, processes, and technology. But people are the ones who write and follow processes. People are the ones who create, configure, and use the technology. People are the most important part of the organization, and they make all the difference when it comes to security. In order for the changes that Zero Trust will require to be sustainable, an organization's culture must be supportive. Security should be integrated into everything that the organization does, from training to weekly departmental meetings. And performing regular tabletop exercises will help bring the organization together to intentionally develop this culture.

Every organization in the world should be doing cybersecurity tabletop exercises just like businesses are required to perform annual fire drills. They are critical to help employees know what to do when something bad happens. The amount of effort it takes to develop a tabletop exercise can vary greatly depending on how complex a scenario will be taken on. A simple tabletop can be based on freely available templates from CISA. MarchFit's MSEL that was used for their tabletop exercise is included in Appendix C. Any tabletop exercise—and especially a live-fire exercise—takes preparation to ensure that the exercise provides real value for the organization. The PZT team spent weeks prior to the event preparing the scenario and developing all the supporting materials to make sure the event went off smoothly.

Some people say security starts from the top down, while others say that it comes from the bottom up. And they're both right. The leaders of MarchFit supported Project Zero Trust and paved the way for its success. The 2021 Verizon Data Breach report indicates that rogue insiders are responsible for 22 percent of all data breaches (www.verizon.com/business/resources/reports/dbir). MarchFit could have been one of those organizations, but the culture of the organization is what allowed Rose to come forward to help catch the hacker without fear of retribution from her boss.

Zero Trust primarily focuses on prevention, and one of the key elements to accomplish this is containment. Containment limits lateral movement inside an organization to other more critical systems through techniques like microsegmentation and least privilege access. Containment can also be accomplished by quickly identifying when resources are impacted by an intrusion, limiting the amount of time a threat actor has on the network to accomplish their objectives.

Because Zero Trust is a strategic initiative, it's important to benchmark your Zero Trust journey and measure how your maturity changes over time after making adjustments to your protect surfaces. The maturity model is based on the standard Capability Maturity Model, which has five stages: (1) Initial, (2) Repeatable, (3) Defined, (4) Managed, and (5) Optimized. For each protect surface, the Zero Trust Maturity Model measures the maturity of each of the five stages of the design methodology. For any given protect surface, each stage of the design methodology could have different levels of maturity, and there should be a strategic plan for improving your Zero Trust maturity based on your risk register and the criticality of the protect surface. In addition, you should take into account the overall view of how all of the protect surfaces interact, because an incident in one could impact others that are a part of the transaction flow.

In the beginning of the story, the Project Zero Trust team was given six months to implement Zero Trust in MarchFit. Six months may seem like a short amount of time, but based on feedback I've received from other cybersecurity leaders who've gone through Zero Trust transformations, six to nine months is actually a good time frame. You shouldn't expect to complete your Zero Trust journey in just a few months. But you do need to be able to demonstrate value in a reasonable period of time to justify the business value to your executive stakeholders. Breaking down your Zero Trust journey into bite-sized pieces can help ensure the long-term success of the initiative. You can use the first phase of a Zero Trust project to build the business case to move on to the next phase. This is where the Zero

Trust Maturity Model can come into play. Your first steps might be from level one to level two, and the following year you can move from stage two to stage three.

"Every Step Matters."

I chose this for MarchFit's creed because it resonates so much with what we do in cybersecurity—and, in particular, Zero Trust. There is a reason for everything we do, and everything we do makes a difference. *Every Step Matters*.

Appendix A
Zero Trust Design Principles and Methodology

The Four Zero Trust Design Principles

1. **Define business outcomes**: Ask the question "What is the business trying to achieve?" This aligns Zero Trust to the grand strategic outcomes of the organization and makes cybersecurity a business enabler instead of the business inhibitor that it is often seen as today.
2. **Design from the inside out**: Start with the data, applications, assets, and services (DAAS) elements and the protect surfaces that need protection and design outward from there.
3. **Determine who or what needs access**: Determine who needs to have access to a resource in order to get their job done. It is very common to give too many users too much access to sensitive data for no business reason.
4. **Inspect and log all traffic**: All traffic going to and from a protect surface must be inspected and logged for malicious content and unauthorized activity, up through Layer 7.

The Five-Step Zero Trust Design Methodology

1. **Define the protect surface**: Identify the DAAS elements: data, applications, assets, and services, that you want to protect.

2. **Map the transaction flows**: Zero Trust is a system, and in order to secure the system, understanding how the network works is imperative to a successful Zero Trust deployment. The mapping of the transaction flows to and from the protect surface shows how various DAAS components interact with other resources on your network and, therefore, where to place the proper controls. The way traffic moves across the network, specific to the data in the protect surface, determines the design.

3. **Build a Zero Trust architecture**: Part of the magic of the five-step model is that the first two steps will illuminate the best way to design the Zero Trust architecture. The architectural elements cannot be predetermined. Each Zero Trust environment is tailor-made for each protect surface. A good rule of thumb in design is to place the controls as close as possible to the protect surface.

4. **Create a Zero Trust policy**: Ultimately, instantiate Zero Trust as a Layer 7 Policy Statement. Therefore, it requires Layer 7 controls. Use the Kipling Method of Zero Trust policy writing to determine who or what can access your protect surface.

5. **Monitor and maintain the environment**: One of the design principles of Zero Trust is to inspect and log all traffic, all the way through Layer 7. The telemetry provided by this process will not just help prevent data breaches and other significant cybersecurity events, but will provide valuable security improvement insights. This means that each protect surface can become more robust and better protected over time. Telemetry from cloud, network, and endpoint controls can be analyzed using advances in behavioral analytics, machine learning, and artificial intelligence to stop attacks in real time and improve security posture over the long term.

Appendix B
Zero Trust Maturity Model

Because Zero Trust is a strategic initiative, it's important to benchmark your Zero Trust journey and measure your improvements over time. The Zero Trust Maturity Model documents improvements made to your individual Zero Trust environments. Designed using a standard Capability Maturity Model, the Zero Trust Maturity Model leverages the five-step methodology for implementing Zero Trust and should be used to measure the maturity of an individual protect surface containing a single DAAS element.

Step	Initial (1)	Repeatable (2)	Defined (3)	Managed (4)	Optimized (5)
	The initiative is undocumented and performed on an ad hoc basis with processes undefined. Success is dependent on individual efforts.	The process is documented and is predictably repeatable, using lessons learned in the initial phase.	Processes for success have been defined and documented.	Processes are monitored and controlled; efficacy is measurable.	The focus is on continuous optimization.
1. Define your protect surface. Determine which single DAAS element will be protected inside the defined protect surface.	The DAAS element is unknown or discovered manually; data classification is not done or is incomplete.	The use of automated tools to discover and classify DAAS elements has begun, but is not standardized.	Data classification training and processes have been introduced and are maturing; protect surface discovery is becoming automated.	New or updated DAAS elements are immediately discovered, classified, and assigned to the correct protect surface in an automated manner.	Discovery and classification processes are fully automated.

2. Map the transaction flows. The mapping of the transaction flows to and from the protect surface shows how various DAAS components interact with other resources on your network and, therefore, where to place the proper controls.	Flows are conceptualized based on interviews and workshops.	Traditional scanning tools and event logs are used to construct approximate flow maps.	A flow mapping process is in place. Automated tools are beginning to be deployed.	Automated tools create precise flow maps. All flow maps are validated with system owners.	Transaction flows are automatically mapped across all locations in real time.
3. Architect a Zero Trust environment. A Zero Trust architecture is designed based upon the protect surface and the interaction of resources based upon the flow maps.	With little visibility and an undefined protect surface, the architecture cannot be properly designed.	Protect surface is established based on current resources and priorities.	The basics of the protect surface enforcement is complete, including placing segmentation gateways in the appropriate places.	Additional controls are added to evaluate multiple variables (e.g., endpoint controls, SAAS, and API controls).	Controls are enforced using a combination of hardware and software capabilities.

4. Create Zero Trust policy. Create Zero Trust policy following the Kipling Method of Who, What, When, Where, Why, and How.	Policy is written at Layer 3.	Additional "who" statements are starting to be identified to address business needs; user IDs of applications and resources are known, but access rights are unknown.	The team works with the business to determine who or what should have access to the protect surface.	Custom user-specific elements are created and defined by policy, reducing policy space and number of users with access.	Layer 7 policy is written for granular enforcement; only known traffic and legitimate application communication are allowed.
5. Monitor and maintain. Telemetry from all controls in the protection chain are captured, analyzed, and used to stop attacks in real time and enhance defenses to create more robust protections over time.	Visibility into what is happening on the network is low.	Traditional SIEM or log repositories are available, but the process is still mostly manual.	Telemetry is gathered from all controls and is sent to a central data lake.	Machine learning tools are applied to the data lake for context into how traffic is used in the environment.	Data is incorporated from multiple sources and used to refine steps 1–4; alerts and analyses are automated.

Appendix C
Sample Zero Trust Master
Scenario Events List

The Master Scenario Events List (MSEL) comes from the NIST Special Publication 800-84 Guide to Test, Training, and Exercise Programs for IT Plans and Capabilities. This standard details all of the aspects of creating, running, and debriefing after a tabletop exercise. The most important part of a tabletop will be the planning—identifying the audience, defining the objectives, and creating a realistic scenario will all help maximize the organization's cybersecurity potential by improving their security incident response plans, identifying potential weaknesses or gaps in controls, and preparing individuals for playing their respective roles during an incident.

The Master Scenario Events List is a timeline of the scripted events to be injected into exercise play by a moderator to generate participant activity based on the objectives identified by the organizers. This script ensures that necessary events happen to generate discussion of policies, procedures, and plans and to help identify weaknesses based on real-world conditions. The MSEL should be used to track participant responses to injects and deviations from expected behaviors and to help reinforce the learning points associated with those actions.

Objective 1—Can the team avoid a disruption to operations during an incident?

Objective 2—Can the team tell the difference between a real issue and a false positive?

Objective 3—Identify any gaps in technology controls, incident response procedures, resources, or training that could impact the organization if this were a real incident.

Inject	Expected Outcome	Learning Points	Maximum (Minutes) for Each Message
"Injects" are events within the scenario that prompt participants to implement the plans, policies, and/ or procedures to be tested during the exercise. Each inject should be considered its own "event" within the timeline of the scenario.	Expected outcomes represent management/ administration's desired responses or actions to the questions or messages proposed during the delivery of injects.	Learning points are the specific takeaways that participants will learn from the inject and discuss afterward.	It is necessary to limit the time for the discussion of each inject so that all injects can be addressed during the given exercise time frame.

Inject	Expected Outcome	Learning Points	Maximum (Minutes) for Each Message
8:35 a.m.: Several customers report to support services that their Tread-March units appear to start, but only display a blue screen and will not connect to the network.	1. Follow/Initiate incident response process with appropriate escalation. 2. Investigate for further information.	Not all incidents are related to hacking.	15 minutes
8:45 a.m.: Security operations center reports suspicious activity on several user accounts. Nothing outside what their accounts are allowed to do.	1. How is suspicious activity detected? 2. How do you define suspicious activity? 3. Review account permissions and recent activity.	Are staff trained to detect suspicious behavior? Is there enough information to correlate events?	15 minutes
9:00 a.m.: Call center reports that call volume is higher than normal for a weekday.	1. Will the team be distracted by the lack of information and jump to the conclusion that a problem is more widespread than it actually is?	Does the organization have operational monitoring of treadmills, operational status, firmware versions, etc. to evaluate trends?	10 minutes

Inject	Expected Outcome	Learning Points	Maximum (Minutes) for Each Message
9:30 a.m.: Technician reinstalls firmware on malfunctioning treadmill. Reports that a security dongle has been missing for several days.	1. What is the appropriate reporting process for lost or stolen equipment? 2. Does identity management allow for fast decommissioning of hardware tokens?	How will incident response team receive communications from impacted teams in real time?	10 minutes
10:07 a.m.: After reviewing account activity, security team member personally knew one of the users and texted to see what they were doing. User is on vacation.	1. Can team communicate with impacted users? 2. Does the organization have adequate monitoring to review activity logs?	Can the organization detect suspicious or anomalous user activity?	15 minutes
10:15 a.m.: PR department indicates social media sources show there may be a protest about labor conditions outside headquarters.	1. Is there a public information plan in place and has team been trained?	Public messaging is an important part of major exercises and PR personnel need to be in the communication path early on.	10 minutes

Inject	Expected Outcome	Learning Points	Maximum (Minutes) for Each Message
10:29 a.m.: CIO is removed from the scenario due to unexpected circumstances.	1. Does the incident response plan account for personnel changes during the response phase?	A streamlined process should include communications "warm hand-off" for incident response leaders.	10 minutes
11:01 a.m.: Logs show successful two-factor authentications for user with suspicious activity. User mistakenly clicked Approve.	1. Are users trained to report mistaken MFA approvals? 2. When does an incident begin to impact business operations?	Mistakes should be something that you prepare for and learn from, not something that you avoid.	15 minutes
11:12 a.m.: SOC detects port-scanning activity originating from the treadmill firmware update server.	1. Are IoT networks trusted to talk to anything in the environment?	Many sophisticated attacks begin with or target IoT or OT networks.	10 minutes

Inject	Expected Outcome	Learning Points	Maximum (Minutes) for Each Message
11:45 a.m.: Protesters gather outside the building to complain about the working conditions in one of the factories where the treadmills are being produced. Media is now onsite.	1. Is the organization prepared to publicly acknowledge a cyberattack? At what point in the incident response plan is this required? 2. When is the organization required to notify customers or other partners?	Acknowledging and being transparent about an incident to protect the community is a better PR strategy than concealment.	10 minutes
12:25 p.m.: In reviewing traffic logs, the network team sees successful connections from the update server to another server . . . the network vulnerability scanning server.	1. Are necessary network logs available to capture lateral movement from server to server? 2. How long are these logs maintained? Do they contain only metadata or are they full packet captures to view payloads?	Would it have been possible to correlate suspicious activity in real time to have proactively prevented this scenario from escalating?	15 minutes

Inject	Expected Outcome	Learning Points	Maximum (Minutes) for Each Message
12:45 p.m.: Several staff members report seeing a drone flying close to the building.	1. Are sensitive areas visible from outside the building? 2. What protective controls might be available for these areas?	Has the organization performed a physical security audit?	10 minutes
1:05 p.m.: Logs show that the scanning server has been sending unknown traffic to nearly every server and client in the organization over the last several hours.	1. What trust relationships are created to facilitate known security activities? 2. How can these permissions be limited?	Do security controls and policy apply equally to all departments in the organization? Or have exceptions been made and are they well known and understood?	15 minutes
Overnight: Incident response firm worked overnight to determine that malware was installed that had a data exfiltration tool.	1. How would the organization determine what data may have been stolen? 2. Does the organization have a retainer with an incident response firm? 3. When is the appropriate time to notify cyber risk insurers?	How does the organization define a breach and when does data exfiltration necessitate victim notifications?	15 minutes

Appendix D
For Further Reading

Standards, Frameworks, and Other Resources

Center for Internet Security: The 18 CIS Critical Security Controls—www.cisecurity
.org/controls/cis-controls-list

Cybersecurity & Infrastructure Security Agency: CISA Tabletop Exercise
Packages—www.cisa.gov/cisa-tabletop-exercises-packages

Executive Order on Improving the Nation's Cybersecurity—www.whitehouse
.gov/briefing-room/presidential-actions/2021/05/12/executive-order-
on-improving-the-nations-cybersecurity

NIST Special Publication 800-53 Revision 5: Security and Privacy Controls
for Information Systems and Organizations—https://doi.org/10.6028/NIST
.SP.800-53r5

NIST Special Publication 800-61 Revision 2: Computer Security Incident Handling Guide—https://doi.org/10.6028/NIST.SP.800-61r2

NIST Special Publication 800-84: Guide to Test, Training, and Exercise Programs
for IT Plans and Capabilities—https://doi.org/10.6028/NIST.SP.800-84

NIST Special Publication 800-171 Revision 2: Protecting Controlled Unclassified Information in Nonfederal Systems and Organizations—https://doi.org/10.6028/NIST.SP.800-171r2

NIST Special Publication 800-207: Zero Trust Architecture—https://doi.org/10.6028/NIST.SP.800-207

OWASP API Security Project—https://owasp.org/www-project-api-security

OWASP Top 10—https://owasp.org/Top10

Case Studies

Adobe's Case Study on Zero Trust—www.youtube.com/watch?v=IGFhMoRXTqg&t=7s

How Akami Implemented a Zero Trust Security Model—www.akamai.com/us/en/multimedia/documents/case-study/how-akamai-implemented-a-zero-trust-security-model-without-a-vpn.pdf

LogRhythm's Journey to Zero Trust—www.youtube.com/watch?v=Fj4ifrMfD8w&feature=emb_logo

Google BeyondCorp Papers

An overview: "A New Approach to Enterprise Security"—https://research.google.com/pubs/pub43231.html

How Google did it: "Design to Deployment at Google"—https://research.google.com/pubs/pub44860.html

Google's front-end infrastructure: "The Access Proxy"—https://research.google.com/pubs/pub45728.html

Migrating to BeyondCorp: "Maintaining Productivity while Improving Security"—https://research.google.com/pubs/pub46134.html

The human element: "The User Experience"—https://research.google.com/pubs/pub46366.html

Secure your endpoints: "Building a Healthy Fleet"—https://ai.google/research/pubs/pub47356

Books

Cyber Warfare—Truth, Tactics, and Strategies. Dr. Chase Cunningham, Packt Publishing, 2020.

Zero Trust Networks. Evan Gilman, Doug Barth, O'Reilly Media, 2017.

Zero Trust Security: An Enterprise Guide. Jason Garbis, Jerry W. Chapman, Apress, 2021.

Hardening Guides

Best Practices for Securing Active Directory—`https://docs.microsoft.com/en-us/windows-server/identity/ad-ds/plan/security-best-practices/best-practices-for-securing-active-directory`

Cisco Router Hardening Guide—`www.cisco.com/c/en/us/support/docs/ip/access-lists/13608-21.html`

Docker Hardening—`https://docs.docker.com/engine/security`

Kubernetes Hardening Guide—`https://media.defense.gov/2021/Aug/03/2002820425/-1/-1/0/CTR_Kubernetes_Hardening_Guidance_1.1_20220315.PDF`

Microsoft Security Baselines—`https://docs.microsoft.com/en-us/windows/security/threat-protection/windows-security-configuration-framework/windows-security-baselines`

Securing Distribution Independent Linux—`www.cisecurity.org/benchmark/distribution_independent_linux`

VMWare Security Hardening Guides—`www.vmware.com/security/hardening-guides.html`

Windows Server Security Documentation—`https://docs.microsoft.com/en-us/windows-server/security/security-and-assurance`

Glossary

Asserted identity   Identity is always an assertion of the abstraction of a user on a network. The identity system "asserts" that a device is generating packets under the control of the asserted.

Attack surface   An attack surface of an organization is made up of all of the different elements where a threat actor can attempt to exploit weaknesses to obtain unauthorized access into an environment. One strategy for security involves reducing your organization's attack surface; however, in practice this is difficult to do since many services require access to the Internet and consequently the whole world can be an attack surface.

Bring your own device (BYOD)   Many organizations allow employees to bring their own consumer devices into the organization to access company resources or services. For many security teams BYOD comes with the challenge of applying security controls to all the various types of personally owned devices.

Cloud access security broker (CASB)   Many organizations are not able to obtain the same visibility into or control over cloud-based services. CASB services use proxies or API integrations to assist security teams with providing security controls into cloud-based services.

Data, applications, assets, and services (DAAS) DAAS is an acronym that stands for data, applications, assets, and services, which define the sensitive resources that should go into individual protect surfaces. DAAS elements include:

- Data—This is sensitive data that can get an organization in trouble if it is exfiltrated or misused. Examples of sensitive data include payment card information (PCI), protected health information (PHI), personally identifiable information (PII), and intellectual property (IP).
- Applications—Typically these are applications that use sensitive data or control critical assets.
- Assets—Assets could include IT (information technology), OT (operational technology), or IoT (Internet of Things) devices such as point-of-sale terminals, SCADA controls, manufacturing systems, and networked medical devices.
- Services—These are sensitive services that are very fragile that your business depends upon. The most common services that should be protected in a Zero Trust manner include DNS, DHCP, Active Directory, and NTP.

Data toxicity Data toxicity is the doctrine that sensitive data becomes "toxic" to your organization if it has been stolen or exfiltrated from your networks or systems into the control of malicious actors. This exfiltration leads to a negative impact on the business. The data has become toxic as its theft leads to lawsuits or regulatory action on the organization. Every organization has both nontoxic and toxic data. An easy way to recognize toxic data types is to remember the 4Ps of toxic data: PCI (credit card data), PII (personally identifiable information), PHI (patient health information), and IP (intellectual property). Most toxic data falls into this simple framework.

DevOps DevOps is a software development philosophy that shortens the software development life cycle by continuously and rapidly deploying software updates and results in higher-quality, more innovative software.

Endpoint detection and response (EDR) The previous generation of antivirus used file hashes as signatures to identify malware, requiring huge amounts of human effort to identify malicious code, but this approach led to attackers modifying code to evade detection. EDR takes a different approach, applying machine learning to identify how malicious code interacts with the operating system and allows investigators to identify and correlate security events on endpoints and take action on those alerts.

Granular access control   Granular access control is the outcome of an explicitly defined Zero Trust Kipling Method Policy statement. Multiple access control criteria provide fine-grained policy for access to a protect surface, making it substantially more difficult to perform a successful attack against that protect surface.

Identity   Identity is the validated and authenticated "who" statement that is part of the Kipling Method Policy assertion: "Who" should have access to a resource?

Identity and Access Management (IAM)   Identity and Access Management are the organization-specific policies and controls that help manage the life cycle of an identity through its journey from creation to removal. Typically there are four areas where organizations manage identities: authentication, authorization, user management, and directory services. In addition, individual identities may inherit permissions from groups, so managing groups of users is also important to an IAM program. The most critical part of an IAM program is the governance of how identities are managed and how policies are created and changed.

Internet of Things (IoT)   Many of the devices on a network today aren't desktops or laptops where a human is the primary source of activity. Cameras, card readers, printers, building control systems, personal mobile devices, personal assistants, TVs, gaming devices, and wearables all may attempt to connect to the company network.

Kipling Method Policy (KMP)   Zero Trust policy is created using the Kipling Method, named after the writer Rudyard Kipling, who gave the world the idea of Who, What, When, Where, Why and How in a poem in 1902. Since the idea of WWWWWH is well known worldwide, it crosses languages and cultures and allows easily created, easily understood, and easily auditable Zero Trust policy statements for various technologies. A KMP determines what traffic can transit the microperimeter at any point in time, preventing unauthorized access to your protect surface, while preventing the exfiltration of sensitive data into the hands of malicious actors. True Zero Trust requires Layer 7 technology to be fully effective. The Kipling Method describes a Layer 7 Zero Trust granular policy.

Using the Kipling Method, you can create Zero Trust policy effortlessly by answering the following questions:

- *Who should be allowed to access a resource?* The validated "asserted identity" will be defined in the Who statement. This replaces the source IP address in a traditional firewall rule.

- *What application is the asserted identity allowed to use to access the resource?* In almost all cases, protect surfaces are accessed via an application. The application traffic should be validated at Layer 7 to keep attackers from impersonating the application at the port and protocol level and using the rule maliciously. The What statement replaces port and protocol designations in traditional firewall rules.
- *When defines a time frame?* When is the asserted identity allowed to access the resource? It is common for rules to be instantiated 24/7, but many rules should be time limited and turned off when authorized users are not typically using the rule. Attackers take advantage of these always-on rules and attack when approved users are away from the system, making the attacks more difficult to discover.
- *Where are the locations from which a resource will be accessed?* Where are the resources located? Where defines the position of a specific location, object, or device. The Where statement replaces the destination IP address in traditional firewall rules. The geolocation of a resource should always be known, and impossible travel rules will alert administrators to spoofing attempts.
- *Why are we protecting this resource?* The classification of a resource as public, private, secret, or top secret should be aligned with the controls. Many applications mix multiple types of data within the same protect surface, so it is critical to have an inventory that includes compliance requirements, privacy impact, intellectual property, and business considerations.
- *How will the resource be protected?* This can include all of the controls that should be applied to the protect surface, including encryption and decryption, URL filtering, sandboxing, signatures, anomaly detection, etc.

Least-privilege access   Least-privilege access asks the question "Does a user need to have access to a specific resource to get their job done?" We give too much access to most users based upon the broken trust model. By mandating a least-privilege, or need-to-know, policy, the ability of a user to perform malicious actions against a resource is severely limited. This mitigates against both stolen credential and insider attacks.

Managed Security Service Provider (MSSP)   Because of the challenges of hiring or retaining security staff, many organizations have turned to MSSPs to provide security consulting, SOC, forensics, and incident response, among other key service needs. One of the main benefits of an MSSP is that it has the ability to correlate data from attacks against hundreds or thousands of customers across various industries. It is important to note, however, that an organization can't outsource the responsibility or accountability of security, so there should be an owner of security inside the organization.

Microperimeter   When a segmentation gateway (SG) connects to a protect surface and a Layer 7 Kipling Method Policy is deployed, then a microperimeter is placed around the protect surface. The microperimeter ensures that only known approved and validated traffic has access to the protect surface, based upon policy. One architectural principle of Zero Trust is to move your SG as close as possible to the protect surface for the most effective preventative controls enforced by the microperimeter.

Microsegmentation   Microsegmentation is the act of creating a small segment in a network so that attackers have difficulty moving around and accessing internal resources. Many networks are "flat," meaning that there are no internal segments, so if an attacker gets a foothold in the network, they can move around unnoticed to attack resources and steal data. A microperimeter is a type of microsegment. The microperimeter defines a Layer 7 boundary for protections of a DAAS element. Some organizations may choose to use Layer 3 microsegmentation technology inside a microperimeter.

National Institute for Standards and Technology (NIST)   NIST is a U.S. government entity that creates and publishes standards across many different industries. The philosophy of NIST is that through creating standards, organizations can better innovate and compete in a global economy. NIST has created a number of indispensable standards when it comes to cybersecurity, including the ones mentioned in this book:

- 800-53—Security and Privacy Controls for Information Systems and Organizations
- 800-61—Computer Security Incident Handling Guide
- 800-84—Guide to Test, Training, and Exercise Programs for IT Plans and Capabilities
- 800-171—Protecting Controlled Unclassified Information in Nonfederal Systems and Organizations
- 800-207—Zero Trust Architecture

Operational technology (OT)   Increasingly, sophisticated threat actors have moved from targeting user desktops or laptops to targeting the control systems that help manage factories, buildings, oil pumps, or smart cities. OT systems interact with the physical environment of an organization and are often a blind spot for security teams.

Policy engine   A policy engine was proposed in NIST SP 800-207 to help focus Zero Trust implementations around the concepts of least privilege and identity. In theory, a policy engine could help organizations provide just-in-time access to resources where authentication is happening continuously.

Privileged access management (PAM)   One of the biggest targets inside an organization are its privileged accounts like Active Directory Domain Admin accounts. If compromised, these accounts can allow an attacker to take any action they choose inside an organization and it becomes increasingly difficult to remove an attacker after they have obtained one of these accounts. PAM tools help protect these accounts and assist organizations in auditing and tracking admin activities to help detect a compromise.

Protect surface   The protect surface is the opposite of an attack surface. An attack surface is massive and includes the entire Internet while a protect surface is limited to systems under your control. A Zero Trust strategy focuses on applying tailored controls to protect surfaces rather than attempting to manage a huge attack surface. Each protect surface contains a single DAAS element. Each Zero Trust environment will have multiple protect surfaces.

Secure Access Services Edge (SASE)   With the rise of remote access required after the onset of the 2020 pandemic, many organizations wanted to ensure that workers could work from anywhere while enforcing the same levels of security on user devices. SASE tools can take many forms but often come as an agent that limits network access to a device based on policy, provides for remote browser isolation when accessing the Internet, proxies access to cloud services.

Secure web gateway (SWG)   One of the most common ways of infecting a computer with malware is to have a user click a malicious web address that downloads malware to the user's computer. SWGs help protect users from visiting these malicious websites by acting as a proxy for outbound user traffic from an organization to enforce company policies.

Security Information Event Management (SIEM)   Threat actors will commonly attempt to hide or destroy any evidence that a system has been compromised. For logs that remain on a compromised system, this is easy for an attacker to accomplish. In response, security teams now send logs to a centralized logging server that maintains a forensically secure copy of these logs in the event an organization experiences a breach. SIEM tools will typically parse and normalize log data that allows these systems to help correlate suspicious activity and alert admins when malicious activity has been detected.

Security Operations Center (SOC)   Many organizations choose to employ a SOC to provide 24x7 monitoring of security telemetry from SIEM systems, network detection and response tools, or API integrations with an organization's, EDR, SOAR, SWG, CASB, PAM, or SASE tools.

Security orchestration, automation, and response (SOAR)   SOCs typically gather inputs from many different sources and require analysts to review information from multiple systems for investigations and then take action in many different additional systems to respond to threats. SOAR systems rely on playbooks designed by organizations to correlate specific types of activity and then create automated responses based on those detections, reducing the time it takes to respond to a threat from hours to seconds.

Segmentation gateway (SG)   A segmentation gateway is a Layer 7 gateway designed to segment networks based upon users, applications, and data. Segmentation gateways are the primary technology used to enforce Layer 7 policy in Zero Trust environments. Segmentation gateways can be physical (PSG) when used in traditional on-premise networks, or virtual (VSG) when used in public or private clouds. Next-generation firewalls traditionally function as segmentation gateways when they are deployed in Zero Trust environments.

Software as a Service (SaaS)   SaaS is the model of selling software that is delivered to a user through a cloud-based platform rather than the typical licensing model of installing the software on a user's computer. The SaaS model has the advantage to customers in terms of speed of delivery, while software companies benefit from only supporting the current version of the software rather than many legacy versions. The challenge of SaaS for security teams is the lack of visibility and control over user activity in this model, and many organizations choose to implement a CASB in order to get this control back.

Trust levels   The existing cybersecurity paradigm is based upon a broken trust model where all systems external to the corporate networks are considered "untrusted" and those inside the corporate networks are known as "trusted." It is this flaw that undergirds Zero Trust. Trust is a human emotion injected into digital systems for no technical reason. It is not measurable. Trust is binary. All successful cyberattacks exploit trust in some manner, making trust a dangerous vulnerability that must be mitigated. In Zero Trust, all packets are untrusted and are treated exactly the same as every other packet flowing across the system. The trust level is defined as zero, hence the term Zero Trust.

Web application firewall (WAF)   A traditional firewall is used to manage policies at an IP or TCP/UDP port level. These traditional firewalls lack awareness of what happens at the application layer of a session and can't protect from web-based attacks like SQL injection or cross-site scripting. In contrast, a WAF operates only at the application layer and provides signature-based rules to stop common OWASP attacks as well as enforcing input validation on sites or detection of credential stuffing attacks where threat actors use compromised passwords to attempt to access sensitive resources.

Zero Trust   Zero Trust is a strategic initiative that helps prevent successful data breaches by eliminating digital trust from your organization. Rooted in the principle of "never trust, always verify," Zero Trust is designed as a strategy that will resonate with the highest levels of any organization yet can be tactically deployed using off-the-shelf technology. Zero Trust strategy is decoupled from technology, so while technologies will improve and change over time, the strategy remains the same.

Zero Trust architecture   Your Zero Trust architecture is the compilation of the tools and technologies used to deploy and build your Zero Trust environment. This technology is fully dependent upon the protect surface you are protecting, as Zero Trust is designed from the inside out, starting at the protect surface and moving outward from there. Typically, the protect surface will be protected by a Layer 7 segmentation gateway that creates a microperimeter that enforces Layer 7 controls with Kipling Method Policy. Every Zero Trust architecture is tailor made for an individual protect surface.

Zero Trust environment   A Zero Trust environment designates the location of your Zero Trust architecture, consisting of a single protect surface containing a single DAAS element. Zero Trust environments are places where Zero Trust controls and policies are deployed. These environments include traditional on-premises networks such as data centers, public clouds, private clouds, endpoints, or across an SD-WAN.

Zero Trust Network Access (ZTNA)   Created by Gartner in 2019, the term ZTNA refers to a category of tools that help facilitate providing secure access to private networks through authenticated access. This term helps broaden the definition of remote access through older technologies like virtual private networks (VPNs) to secure web gateways (SWGs) or Secure Access Service Edge (SASE) agents.

Index

A

access, determining, 165
access reviews, 69
alert fatigue, 100
API keys, 79
application programming interfaces
(APIs), 109–110, 115, 162
applications
application logs, 50, 54
cloud, 103–116
deploying, 113
legacy, 65
scalability of, 113
security of, 83

B

badges, 39
BAS (breach and attack simulation),
155
best of breed, 26

best practices, 46
blind spots, 95, 105, 114–115
blue team, 134
Box, 114
breach and attack simulation
(BAS), 155
buffer overflows, 144
bug bounty programs, 85
Business Continuity Plan (BCP), 28, 46
Business Impact Assessment (BIA), 28
business outcomes, 165

C

cameras, 161
Capability Maturity Model,
154, 163, 167
card reader, 30, 31, 33, 34, 36, 38,
39–41, 161
CASB (Cloud Access Security Broker),
95, 107, 114, 162

CCPA, 71
Centola, David, 130
challenge questions, 65
Chang, Donna, 5
CIAQ (Consensus Assessments Initiative Questionnaire), 106
CI/CD (continuous integration and continuous delivery), 76–77, 79
Cloud Access Security Broker (CASB), 95, 107, 114, 162
cloud apps, 103–116
cloud logging, 95
cloud security, 120
Cloud Security Alliance, 106, 115, 120
cloud services, 162
CMDB tools, 100
code review, 82
collaboration tools, 122, 123
compliance, 26
compliance-management mechanisms, 50, 54
Consensus Assessments Initiative Questionnaire (CIAQ), 106
Consumer Identity and Access Management, 161
container checks, 111
containment, 32, 163
Containment, Eradication, and Recovery stage, of NIST Cybersecurity Framework, 99–100
containment, measuring, 96, 101
continuous integration and continuous delivery (CI/CD), 76–77, 79
contracts, 106
Covey, Stephen
  Speed of Light, 131
credentialed scan, 145, 148–149

cross-site scripting (XSS), 84–85, 114–115
culture of security. *See* sustainable culture
Cunningham, Chase, 7
Curphey, Mark, 78
cyber insurance carrier, 142–143

D
data, applications, assets, and services (DAAS) elements, 165, 167
data-driven decisions, 44
deception technologies, 155
defense in depth, 26
Defined stage
  of Capability Maturity Model, 163
  of Zero Trust Maturity Model, 168–170
deploying applications/services, 113
DevOps, 73–85, 161
disaster recovery tools, 100
Docker, 84

E
emulation tools, 155
Equifax, 115–116
ERP change control, 49, 54
ERP systems, 50, 52, 53, 54, 161
error pages, 108
Experian, 115–116

F
Facebook, 115
false positives, 135
feedback loop, 101
firewalls, 32, 80
fog of war, 149
Forrester, 54

G
Gartner, 54
General Data Protection Regulation
    (GDPR), 59–60, 71
Google, 54
Groves, Dennis, 78

H
HIPAA, 71
honeypots, 96, 157
honeytokens, 96
hotwash, 143
human behavior, 130

I
IaaS (infrastructure as a code), 81
identity
    about, 50
    as a cornerstone, 57–72
    importance of, 161
Identity Defined Security Alliance
    (IDSA), 69, 72
incident management, 41
incident response (IR) process, 97, 99,
    100, 101–102
Information Security Advisory
    Council (ISAC), 123
infrastructure as a code (IaaS), 81
Initial stage
    of Capability Maturity Model, 163
    of Zero Trust Maturity
        Model, 168–170
inside-out design, 109
intellectual property, 76
internal network, 32
inventory, 160
IoT devices, 144, 148
IP addresses, 88–89, 123–124

IR (incident response) process, 97, 99,
    100, 101–102
ISAC (Information Security Advisory
    Council), 123
ISO 27001, 98

J
Jacobson, Lenore, 131

K
Kindervag, John, 7, 51, 71, 92, 154, 159
Kubernetes, 79–80, 84, 110–111

L
legacy applications, 65
live-fire drill, 135, 148
Lockheed Martin Cyber Kill Chain,
    59

M
Managed Security Service Provider
    (MSSP), 91, 93, 101, 161–162
Managed stage
    of Capability Maturity Model, 163
    of Zero Trust Maturity
        Model, 168–170
Master Scenario Events List (MSEL),
    135, 147, 171–177
maturity model, 163
memory-safe IoT programming
    language, 144
MFA (multifactor authentication),
    64–65, 68, 107–108, 113, 123
microsegmentation, 40–41
MITRE ATT&CK framework,
    94, 96, 156
MITRE Engage framework, 156–157
monitoring, 68–69, 95, 166, 170

MSEL (Master Scenario Events List), 135, 147, 171–177
MSSP (Managed Security Service Provider), 91, 93, 101, 161–162
multifactor authentication (MFA), 64–65, 68, 107–108, 113, 123

N
National Institute of Standards and Technology (NIST)
   definition of Zero Trust (ZT), 55
   NIST Cybersecurity Framework, 98, 99, 102
   SP 800-53, 98
   SP 800-61, 99, 102
   SP 800-84 Guide to Test, Training, and Exercise Programs for IT Plans and Capabilities, 135, 147, 171
   SP 800-171, 98
   SP 800-207, 51, 54–55, 108, 109, 114, 161
   Zero Trust network view, 52
Network Detection and Response (NDR) tools, 95
network segmentation, 80
network-based detection, 95
networked devices, 40

O
OneDrive, 107, 114
Open Supervised Device Protocol (OSDP), 34
Open Web Application Security Project (OWASP), 77–78, 79, 84, 109, 114–115
Optimized stage

of Capability Maturity Model, 163
of Zero Trust Maturity Model, 168–170
OSDP (Open Supervised Device Protocol), 34
OWASP (Open Web Application Security Project), 77–78, 79, 84, 109, 114–115

P
PAM (privileged access management), 64
Park, Chun, 117
Parler, 115
password vault, 124
passwords
   reusing, 124
   storing, 83
patches, 47, 76–77, 101–102
Peloton, 115
people, as the weakest link, 131, 162
perimeter security, 31–33
The Phoenix Project, 76
physical security, 31–33, 39, 160–161
policy enforcement point, 108–109
policy engine, 114
port scan, 148
privileged access management (PAM), 64
problem management, 41
protect surfaces, 93, 97, 98, 100, 104, 105, 113, 120, 128, 154, 163, 165, 166, 168
provisioning accounts, 60–63
proximity badges, 40
proximity card system, 33

PSExec, 89, 90
purchase orders, 106
purple team, 134
Pygmalion effect, 127, 131

R
RBAC (role-based access control), 80
reauthentication, 66
red herrings, 149
red team, 134
Repeatable stage
    of Capability Maturity Model, 163
    of Zero Trust Maturity
        Model, 168–170
RFID cloner, 39
rightsizing exercise, 154
risk register, 160, 163
role cleanup, 68
role-based access control (RBAC), 80
Rosenthal, Robert, 131
Rust, 144

S
SaaS (software-as-a-service),
    106–107, 115
SalesForce, 114
scalability, of applications/
    services, 113
SDP (software-defined perimeter),
    108–109, 114
secondary attack surface, 32
Secure Access Services Edge (SASE),
    109, 110, 114
Secure Service Edge (SSE), 109
security
    cloud, 120
    as code, 110–111

perimeter, 31–33
physical, 31–33, 39, 160–161
security awareness training, 125, 130
security dongle, 139
security guards, 41
security information and event man-
    agement (SIEM) system, 53, 69
security minute, 124–125
Security Operations Center (SOC),
    87–102, 161–162
security orchestration system, 93, 94
segmentation, 145
shadow IT, 113–114
Shared Assessments, 115
SharePoint, 107, 114, 130
Shift Left philosophy, 94
SIEM (security information and event
    management) system, 53, 69
SIM-jacking, 60
Single Sign On (SSO), 83, 122–123
Slack, 130
SOC (Security Operations Center),
    87–102, 161–162
software-as-a-service (SaaS),
    106–107, 115
software-defined perimeter (SDP),
    108–109, 114
SolarWinds breach, 65–66
specialized programming languages,
    49, 54
Speed of Light (Covey), 131
SQL injection, 78, 84–85, 114–115
SSE (Secure Service Edge), 109
SSO (Single Sign On), 83, 122–123
standards, 110–111, 147
strategy, Zero Trust as a, 13–28
sustainable culture, 117–131

T

tabletop exercise, 133–149, 162
tactics, techniques, and procedures
    (TTPs), 100–101, 156
teams, implementing, 160
technology silos, 159
telemetry, 166
traditional vulnerability management
    tools, 49, 54
traffic
    inspecting and logging, 165
    unknown, 160
transaction flow matrix chart,
    154–155
transaction flows, 36–37, 39,
    47–49, 166, 169
trust
    compared with Zero Trust,
        10–11
    as a vulnerability, 29–41
TTPs (tactics, techniques, and
    procedures), 100–101, 156

U
UEBA, 52, 69
uncredentialed scan, 145
unknown traffic, 160

V
Vega, Victor, 73
vendors, 106
Verizon Data Breach report
    (2021), 163
virtual local area network (VLAN),
    40

vulnerability, trust as a, 29–41
vulnerability scanning server, 144–145,
    148–149

W
web application firewalls (WAFs),
    80–81, 84–85, 107–108, 109,
    114–115, 162
wellness program, 125–126

X
XSS (cross-site scripting),
    84–85, 114–115

Z
Zero Trust (ZT)
    architecture for, 166, 169
    case for, 1–11
    challenges of, 56
    compared with trust, 10–11
    defined, 55
    design principles, 16, 18, 27, 30–31,
        51, 92, 159, 165
    DevOps, 73–85
    implementation curve, 27–28
    methodology, 18, 27, 159, 166
    policy for, 166, 170
    SOC, 87–102
    as a strategy, 13–28
    sustainable culture, 117–131
    tabletop exercise, 133–149
    tenets of, 55
    trap to, 131
Zero Trust Enterprise (ZTE), 55
Zero Trust Maturity Model, 153–154,
    167–170